EVERY
PROMISE
FULFILLED

LITERARY
CURRENTS
IN
BIBLICAL
INTERPRETATION

EDITORS

Danna Nolan Fewell
Perkins School of Theology,
Southern Methodist University, Dallas TX
David M. Gunn
Columbia Theological Seminary, Decatur GA

EDITORIAL ADVISORY BOARD

Jack Dean Kingsbury
Union Theological Seminary in Virginia, Richmond VA
Peter D. Miscall
St Thomas Seminary, Denver CO
Gary A. Phillips
College of the Holy Cross, Worcester MA
Regina M. Schwartz
Department of English, Duke University, Durham NC
Mary Ann Tolbert
The Divinity School, Vanderbilt University, Nashville TN

EVERY PROMISE FULFILLED

contesting plots in joshua

L. DANIEL HAWK

•

WESTMINSTER/JOHN KNOX PRESS
Louisville, Kentucky

EVERY PROMISE FULFILLED:
CONTESTING PLOTS IN JOSHUA

© 1991 L. Daniel Hawk

First edition

Published by Westminster/John Knox Press,
Louisville, Kentucky

PRINTED IN THE UNITED STATES OF AMERICA
2 4 6 8 9 7 5 3 1

Library of Congress Cataloging-in-Publication Data

Hawk, L. Daniel (Lewis Daniel Hawk). 1955–
Every promise fulfilled : contesting plots in Joshua / L. Daniel Hawk.
— 1st ed.
    p.   cm. — (Literary currents in biblical interpretation)
Includes bibliographical references and indexes.
ISBN 0-664-25235-4

1. Bible. O.T. Joshua—Criticism, interpretation, etc. I. Title.
II. Series.
BS1295.2.H39 1991
222'.2066—dc20   91-30011

To Linda

CONTENTS

SERIES
PREFACE

New currents in biblical interpretation are emerging. Questions about origins—authors, intentions, settings—and stages of composition are giving way to questions about the literary qualities of the Bible, the play of its language, the coherence of its final form, and the relations between text and readers.

Such literary criticism is rapidly acquiring sophistication as it learns from major developments in secular critical theory, especially in understanding the instability of language and the key role of readers in the production of meaning. Biblical critics are being called to recognize that a plurality of readings is an inevitable and legitimate consequence of the interpretive process. By the same token, interpreters are being challenged to take responsibility for the theological, social, and ethical implications of their readings.

Biblical interpretation is changing on the practical as well as the theoretical level. More readers, both inside and outside the academic guild, are discovering that the Bible in literary perspective can powerfully engage people's lives. Communities of faith where the Bible is foundational may find that literary criticism can make the Scripture accessible in a way that historical criticism seems unable to do.

Within these changes lie exciting opportunities for all who seek contemporary meaning in the ancient texts. The goal of the series is to encourage such change and such search, to breach the confines of traditional biblical criticism, and to open channels for new currents of interpretation.

—THE EDITORS

PREFACE

The writing of this book has been enhanced and supported by many who have played important roles in my own story. My thanks go first to David Gunn, whose insight has so shaped my own and whose enthusiasm I found to be a constant source of refreshment. I also ackowledge my indebtedness to Joel and Sandy Downing, whose support, both material and spiritual, has been constant and selfless. Special thanks are due as well to Gene Tucker and Robert Detweiler for many helpful comments and suggestions.

To my parents, Lewis and Barbara Hawk, I express my deep appreciation for their continual encouragement and unwavering support. Most of all, I am grateful for the patience and love unselfishly given me by my wife Linda and affectionately dedicate this book to her.

—L. DANIEL HAWK

EVERY
PROMISE
FULFILLED

1

INTRODUCTION

The story of Joshua is at once a story of endings and beginnings. It tells how the people of Israel came to possess the land promised to their ancestors, thus bringing to a conclusion the promises and expectations propelling Israel's story from early in Genesis. Yet by relating the nation's first experiences in the land the book also signals a new trajectory that will take the larger story beyond Joshua into Judges, Samuel and Kings. Between the book's own beginning and end an important transformation takes place. Wandering Israel outside the land becomes settled Israel at rest within it.

The extent of this transformation and rest is, however, less than settled. Much of the story depicts a *blitzkrieg* in which the repeatedly victorious Israelites conquer the entire land of Canaan (10:28-42; 11:12-23; 12:7-24; 21:43-45; 23:9-10; 24: 11-13). Elsewhere, in contrast, Israel's failure to exterminate the indigenous inhabitants is related (9:14-27; 11:19, 22; 15:63; 16:10; 17:11-12; 19:47). Likewise, the reader meets an Israel eager to obey the commands of Yahweh given through Moses (1:16-18; 4:10; 8:30-35; 24:16-18, 21) but also an Israel slow to respond to Yahweh's directives (18:1-10) and unwilling or unable to execute them (2:1-21; 7:1; 9:1-27; 24:19-20). Taken as a whole, the text's repeated juxtaposition of contrary reports and assertions can be baffling. How much of the land does Israel actually take? Does Israel respond appropriately to Yahweh's commandments?

Historical-critical scholars have generally understood the book's incoherence as a consequence of a complex history of composition; conflicting accounts of Israel's entry into Canaan are to be attributed to different sources and perspectives. The historical-critical consensus holds that diverse materials were assembled, revised, and incorporated into an expansive deuter-onomistic program.[1] In the hands of the editor(s) the source materials were "largely rewritten in such a way that they present the relation between Israel and Joshua, between Joshua and Yahweh, in exemplary and idealistic terms" (Boling 1982: 150). The product of this process is a document which depicts "a golden epoch in which the Israelites worship Jahweh and therefore win brilliant victories within the area of conquest" (Weinfeld 1967:113). Joshua therefore provides narrative confirmation of the deuteronomistic agenda. As Wenham (1971:41) writes,

> The message of the book of Joshua seems to be that Israel was careful by and large to fulfill its covenant obligations and that this is why it enjoyed the blessings conditional on obedience and was able to conquer the promised land.

From a compositional perspective, then, the contradictions in Joshua arise from a clash between deuteronomistic assertions and the unedited claims of original sources or additional materials. If one reads Joshua as a unit, however, this interpretation is problematic. The "golden epoch" reading addresses but one aspect of the book and must dispense with significant portions of the text. The so-called deuteronomistic elements are privileged and the tensions presented by contrary perspectives glossed.[2]

Literary analysis of Joshua is still in the initial phase. The few studies undertaken, such as the structuralist interpretation of Polzin (1980) and the more recent readings of Gunn (1987a) and Eslinger (1989),[3] have demonstrated rich potential. Our reading also adopts a literary approach but with a different focus. As already noted, the book's tensions and contradictions arise either because contrary events are juxtaposed or because the events narrated and the narrator's evaluation of these events are inconsistent. In other words, the reader's sense of textual incongruity is a result of the way the story's events are organized and interpreted; it is a circumstance of the story's *plot.* By confining our reading to matters of plot, we may see more clearly how the configuring of the story gives rise to its tensions and thus develop a strategy for understanding them.

The conventional notion of plot can be traced to Aristotle's definition in *The Poetics.* He described plot as "the imitation of an action . . . the arrangement of the incidents" (1986:27). Working from the tragic and epic genres of his time, he conceived of plot as a singular pattern which unites events into an apprehensible whole. This concept of plot, expanded by subsequent generations of critics and applied to all forms of narrative, continues to undergird the concept of plot as the "outline of events" (Scholes and Kellogg 1966:12).[4]

Biblical critics have used this classical notion of plot to identify compositional units within the biblical text. Claus Westermann (1984), for example, has suggested that narratives create a *Geschehensbogen*, an arc of tension that moves from a beginning through an apex to a resolution (approximating Aristotle's assertion that plot organizes events into a beginning, middle, and end), and uses this scheme to determine the original narrative units in the Genesis stories.[5] Aristotle's influence can also be detected in Gunkel (1901), who describes the storytellers' technique in terms of the Aristotelian values of singularity, unity, verisimilitude, and priority of action.

Recent interest in narrative poetics has encouraged the notion of plot as an aspect of the text's surface structure. Structuralism in particular reduces plot to paradigms of "functions" or patterns of sequences which are defined by the conventions of a specific linguistic system. From this perspective, plot is viewed as the structuring operation by which events are organized according to a particular code. Narrative critics have generally been concerned with the logic and pattern by which plot links events into structures, and with the techniques by which narrative exploits the human experience of temporality.[6]

For the most part, literary critics of biblical narrative have assumed a similar notion of plot, although discussion of plot *per se* has been limited. The narrative studies of Alter (1981), Sternberg (1985), and Bar-Efrat (1989) each discuss aspects of plot to a different extent. Alter's discussion of the literary devices employed in biblical narrative includes many of those characteristic of plot (such as narrative tempo and repetition). Sternberg alludes to plot more frequently and operates from a more explicitly Aristotelian framework. His concept of plot includes Aristotle's assertion of the two lines of dramatic change effected by plot: from happiness to unhappiness and from ignorance to knowledge.[7] Bar-Efrat discusses plot at some length, with numerous illustrations from the biblical text. His concise definition (1989:93) articulates the formalist notions held by many literary critics:

> The plot serves to organize events in such a way as to arouse the reader's interest and emotional involvement, while at the same time imbuing the events with meaning.

Aristotle's concept of plot as a singular unifying pattern has provided the basic framework for contemporary definitions of plot. Yet, the wholesale application of the Aristotelian paradigm to all forms of narrative is open to question. *The Poetics* is concerned with an analysis of Greek tragedy and (to a lesser extent) epic, narrative forms that incorporated particular cultural conventions of homogeneity, cohesion, and singularity. By expanding Aristotle's analysis to address all kinds of narrative, literary critics have essentially worked against Aristotle's deductive program; a general understanding of all narrative has been induced from that applied to a few specific forms.

The formalist notion of plot works well when used to analyze narrative forms that exhibit conventions of singularity and coherence (such as folk tales or 19th-century novels). But what of narratives that do not display coherence and simple linear development? What about more complex narratives—those which exhibit several major plot lines or which present the reader with a series of seeming contradictions? How is one to deal with narratives that, for one reason or another, run counter to conventional expectations of completeness or closure?[8]

Many current approaches to literature challenge the assumption that meaning is simply inherent in the text. They point instead to the reader's role in the production of meaning (as in reader-response criticism), the human perceptions and experiences which underlie the text (as in phenomenological criticism), and the transactional dynamic which occurs between text and reader (as in psychoanalytic criticism).[9] These approaches have enabled critics to rethink traditional concepts of plot, so that attention may be given to the configuring processes by which human beings construct coherent structures of meaning. This leads to more questions. What lies behind the impulse to organize reality into definite and concordant wholes? Why do "our minds inveterately seek structure" in a presentation of events, even if we must provide it ourselves (Chatman 1978:45)? What is the relationship between the constructs which the text presents and those which the reader forms?

Such questions suggest the possibility of speaking about plot on a number of different levels. At the surface level, plot may refer to the framework of a story. A more detailed analysis, however, may understand plot as the arrangement of incidents and patterns as they relate to each other. A more abstract notion of plot, moreover, may refer to plot as "an underlying structure which is to be understood less in terms of the incidents or elements it organizes and more in terms of the mind that does the organizing" (Egan 1978:455).

It will be important to keep all three of these levels of plot in mind as we trace the plot(s) of Joshua. In the most general sense, a plot is easy to discern. The book tells the story of Israel as the people shifted from landless existence outside Canaan to settlement and possession of the land. Yet once the reader moves beyond this level of observation, it becomes a more difficult matter to determine a single thread of coherence. What is the book about? Israel's successful possession of Canaan? Its privileged relationship with Yahweh? Is it about Israel's failure to take the land, or its reckless disregard for the commandments of Yahweh? And what of the jarring inconsistencies one encounters throughout the book?

This reading of Joshua will explore the patterns rendered by the story, as well as the agendas which underlie them. To start, the next chapter summarizes various concepts of plot and introduces the method for analyzing plot in Joshua. The third chapter focuses on two summary texts as paradigms of how plot operates in the book. The fourth chapter traces plot lines which deal with Israel's obedience and disobedience to the words of Moses and the commands of Yahweh. The fifth chapter, in like fashion, explores plot lines that render the story in terms of Israelite integrity and fragmentation, especially as these plot lines address desires for fulfillment. The sixth chapter examines the final section of Joshua (22-24), where the tensions within the book are made explicit through a series of events. The concluding chapter offers a summary and reflects on the nature of Israel's story as presented in Joshua.

Joshua has generally been read for the historical information it may yield rather than for the richness of its story. This reading strategy has significantly hindered appreciation of its rhetorical power. The reader attuned to its rhetoric will discover a remarkable story that exemplifies the tension between the structuring operations of dogma and the circumstances of experience.

2

ELEMENTS
OF
THE
PLOT

I mmediately preceding the account of Jericho's destruction is a
brief but uncanny incident, an encounter between Joshua and
a solitary figure (Josh 5:13-15). Joshua sees a man, with sword
unsheathed, standing in his way. As a sentry might, he approaches the man and issues a challenge: "Are you for us or for
our adversaries?" The man's reply is enigmatic: "No. But I, the
commander of the army of Yahweh, have now come." It is an
unexpectedly evasive response, and yet it is highly significant.
The man's self-identification transforms Joshua's challenge into
a question of theological import; the "you" being addressed is
Yahweh's emissary. Without realizing it, Joshua has inquired
whether Yahweh has chosen to side with Israel.

Upon learning the man's identity, Joshua falls to the ground
and does obeisance. The tone of his second question is far
different: "What is my lord saying to his servant?" Again, the
commander's response is terse: "Take your shoes off your feet,
for the place on which you are standing is holy." The episode
ends abruptly with the report that Joshua did what he was told.

What a strange episode! It is perplexing for a number of
reasons. For one thing, the commander's response does not
properly address Joshua's initial question. Joshua asks the man
to choose one of two alternatives ("Are you for us or for our

adversaries?"), but the answer is a refusal to do so. The simple "No" is noncommittal. Moreover, the story seems to end in mid-course. It is the eve of a great campaign. Is there no further communication? How does the encounter end?

Many commentators have answered such questions by noting the vignette's similarities to the call of Moses (Exod 3:1ff). Numerous points of correspondence link Joshua's experience to that of Moses. For one, the contexts are similar (an unexpected meeting with Yahweh at the beginning of a mission).[1] As in Moses' encounter, Joshua is told that he is standing on holy ground and is directed to remove his shoes. The command itself, furthermore, virtually repeats Yahweh's command to Moses in Exod 3:5.

Given these connections, commentators have generally understood the incident as an affirmation of Joshua and Israel. Most believe it to be a modified folktale or liturgy intended to elevate Joshua and confirm him as Moses' divinely-appointed successor. This view allows a number of interpretations. The story may tell of Joshua's divine commissioning for leadership in the wars of Canaan (Soggin 1972:76-78), or it may affirm Yahweh's sanction of and participation in the holy war (Miller & Tucker 1974:49-50). The encounter may be a test for Joshua, confirming both Joshua's commission and his readiness for the task at hand (Butler 1983:57, 61-62).

There are, however, problems with these readings. First, such views assume that the man with the unsheathed sword presents a positive and supportive image—Yahweh's commander has appeared ready for battle on behalf of Israel. Yet there are reasons to regard the man as an ominous and threatening apparition. In other contexts, a divine being with an unsheathed sword represents death and judgment, not encouragement. In the case of Balaam's encounter, for example, the sword held by the angel of Yahweh has been unsheathed in order to slay the prophet (Num 22:21-35), while David sees a similar apparition during the plague Yahweh sends upon Jerusalem (1 Chron 21:14-16).

Second, the notion that the text has been inserted at this point to reassert that Yahweh is participating in the events makes the entire vignette gratuitous and redundant. Yahweh's promise to be with Israel is repeatedly and emphatically affirmed at the beginning of the book (1:5-9) and is further confirmed by Yahweh's wondrous stoppage of the Jordan (4:21-24).

Positive readings of this vignette generally overlook the many ambiguities it creates. The commander's menacing appearance, his evasive answer to Joshua's initial question, and the episode's abrupt ending all lend an uncanny and ominous tone to the encounter.

For the reader, one of the episode's more unsettling aspects is no doubt its failure to offer a sense of closure. The story seems to end mid-course, leaving one with the sense that there is a good deal more to be told. The conclusion "occurs not under the restraining influence of the friction of the language of the text but in the expanding space of the reader's mind" (Magness 1986:23). Such a suspended ending works on the reader, who continues to ponder possible conclusions in order to close the text's open-endedness.

As noted above, there are explicit connections between Moses' encounter with the burning bush and Joshua's encounter with the commander. Yet Joshua's story is truncated. What happens next? Is this all there is?

When Josh 5:13-15 is read against the story of Moses' call in Exod 3:1ff, the suspension of its ending becomes a glaring omission. After commanding Moses to remove his shoes, Yahweh makes the following declaration concerning Israel:[2]

> I have come down to deliver them from the hand of Egypt and to bring them up from that land to a good and wide land, flowing with milk and honey, to the place of the Canaanites, the Hittites, the Amorites, the Perizzites, the Hivites, and the Jebusites. (Exod 3:8)

The connections with Moses' story encourage the reader to see Josh 5:13-15 as a repetition of the call of Moses, with Joshua in the place of his predecessor. In Joshua's case, however, the divine instruction is cut short at a crucial moment, immediately before the promise of the land is affirmed. In other words, what is left unsaid—what is missing—*is precisely that part of Yah-*

weh's speech that pertains to the present situation. Yahweh's call to Moses affirms deliverance and promise. Since Joshua's encounter follows the same pattern, the reader might expect similar affirmations. A declaration of Yahweh's intent to act on Israel's behalf, along with a reaffirmation of the promise of land, would be singularly appropriate on this, the eve of Israel's first campaign in Canaan. Yet the story ends abruptly without such confirming words, leaving the reader to ponder whether the promise remains in place.

Yahweh's failure to affirm the promise of the land, along with the commander's refusal to commit for Israel, produces a sense of confusion and discordance. The episode is profoundly disturbing. The central issues which the book addresses are brought before the reader, but they are left unanswered. Is Yahweh for Israel or is the divine commitment in question? Will the Israelites indeed experience the fulfillment of Yahweh's promise to bring them into the land?

Why does the story of Israel's entry into Canaan contain such a disturbing episode? This is a question we will ask many times over as we explore the text of Joshua. The book of Joshua, like the commander of Yahweh's army, is an enigma. As a rule, readers expect a narrative text to offer a coherent presentation of events. But such coherence is not so obvious in this story of conquests and settlements. Joshua plays with the reader's sense that reality is coherent—a sense that narrative orchestrates. The book teases the reader with affirmations of coherence and then dismantles the coherence it has rendered. The reader is caught within the tension. How do the pieces fit?

JOSHUA AS NARRATIVE LITERATURE

Narrative is the vehicle by which meaning is communicated in the book of Joshua. Although many units in the book are not narrative in genre—there are speeches and lists and summaries—narrative nevertheless provides the framework into which all material in the book is incorporated. It makes the connections which underscore the relationships and significance of its components. The narrative mode provides temporal orientation for the individual events presented in Joshua, and clarifies them in relation to those which precede and follow.

Narrative organizes temporal experience and provides the structures of coherence and order necessary to integrate and transmit ideologies and experiences. A ubiquitous form of human expression, it constitutes a "human universal by which messages about the nature of shared reality can be transmitted" (White 1980:6).[3] In other words, narrative is a way of making sense of human existence. Our explanations for that which is discordant and unanswerable are expressed through narrative presentation, whether it is an ancient storyteller's account of the creation of earth or an astrophysicist's account of the "big bang."

Reality is generally experienced as an endless sequence of events, many of which appear random, haphazard, and unconnected. In order to create and maintain a sense of integrity, the human psyche makes connections between events, plotting them according to a temporal grid.[4] This cognitive organization of time may be intentional, as in keeping an appointment book, or relatively unconscious, as in the performance of daily routines. In any case, the impulse to organize reality and discern patterns in experience is compelling. Even when no explanation for events is discernable, one is often given to assume the operation of some transcendental design ("Why me?" or "Somebody up there likes me!").

Narrative provides a scheme by which time can be measured and quantified, enabling the connection of events and facilitating the construction of concords. It offers a framework that "demarcates, encloses, establishes limits, orders" (Brooks 1984:4), and thus gives a sense of closure to the open-endedness of time. Through the presentation of order, narrative creates a sense of meaning, so that the events of life can be invested with coherence, plenitude, and significance. It therefore comprises, as Paul Ricoeur has suggested, an essentially mimetic activity, by which life's events find coherence and explanation through configurations which render reality as an apprehensible whole.[5] We read narratives, then, with the expectation that they will display coherence and concordance,

25

that everything will somehow fit within the whole. Narrative reinforces the conviction that "somehow, in some occult fashion, if we could only detect it, everything will be found to hang together" (Kermode 1979:72).

ASPECTS OF PLOT

In exploring the ways narrative shapes experience, many critics have found it useful to adopt the distinction between "story" (*fabula*) and "plot" (*sjužet*) suggested by Russian critics earlier in this century. In this model, the term "story" refers to the raw material of narrative, that which can be abstracted from the narrative and reconstructed in its original chronological sequence. "Plot" refers to the way this material is then presented in its finished form, the order of events as they are encountered. In simple terms, story refers to *what* is depicted, while plot refers to *how* it is depicted.[6] In speaking of plot, then, one is referring to the configurational aspect of narrative—that property of narrative which gives the impression of a continuity and connection between events in time. Plot is "what shapes a story and gives it a certain direction or intent of meaning" (Egan 1978:461).

The operation of plot on story can be illustrated by comparing Joshua's and Josephus' respective renderings of Israel's acquisition of the promised land. Joshua presents a number of disturbing episodes (for example, Israel's spies spend their first night in Canaan in the house of a prostitute) and often exhibits temporal or geographical ambiguity. Josephus' story, on the other hand, is less controversial (Rahab is an innkeeper) and offers precise temporal and geographical settings for the events it relates. Some events are expanded by Josephus (Phinehas offers a long and noble speech to the eastern tribes), while others, significant in Joshua, are neglected (Joshua's speeches in Joshua 23-24 are not recounted). Josephus' story is harmonious and orderly, with little sense of the confusion, disorder, and theological tensions elicited by the biblical account.

The dynamic quality of plot is not, however, confined to the text. The concord-making impulse is also at work in the reader, who likewise exercises a tendency to organize and make connections between events. A narrative therefore elicits a dynamic interpretative relationship between text and reader.

This dynamic has been described by Ricoeur (1984:52-81), who perceives the operation of plot in terms of a three-fold *mimesis*.[7] In his model, mimetic activity is grounded in "prefiguration" (mimesis$_1$), the preunderstanding of symbol and structure which forms the conceptual framework for the composition of plot. From this preunderstanding, the configurational process links the events of story into a unified whole. Through this "emplotment" (mimesis$_2$), a logic is established that makes the pattern of events "followable." This stage of mimesis encompasses all the artifices an author employs to imitate human action, as well as the genres and traditions that make the narrative appear plausible and significant to the audience. Finally, at the intersection of the text and reader a "refiguration" occurs (mimesis$_3$), during which the reader actualizes the paradigms and configuration presented by the narrative.

Although Ricoeur prefers to confine the term "plot" to the actual configurational activity denoted by mimesis$_2$, his scheme is useful in clarifying the dynamic that occurs in the production of plots. At the pole of composition, a narrative draws on paradigms and conventions of understanding in order to select the most appropriate devices and categories to transmit the story, rendering "a network of clues to the speaker's intention" (Sternberg 1985:9). The reader in turn is able to follow a narrative because he or she has acquired the competence to understand and interpret the fundamental principles by which narrative operates—the meanings of verbal tenses, the logic involved in the connection of events, and so on. The reader responds to the clues provided by the text to fill in the gaps and construct hypotheses of understanding.[8] These hypotheses are, in effect, the reader's plots, his or her evaluations of textual events and their connections. Thus an understanding of plot as a dynamic phenomenon goes beyond the formal aspects of the text and addresses the interpretive processes that take place between text and reader.

Plot, then, can be understood as both verb and noun. As verb, it denotes the configuring activity by which story is produced and understood. As noun, it refers to the structures and connections which result from that activity. How plot operates can be further understood by a closer description of its aspects. First, plot elicits a *design* or pattern by which events may be understood. Second, plot addresses the human experience of *temporality*—plot orients events in *time*. Finally, to employ Kermode's oft-quoted phrase, plot elicits *the sense of an ending*—it presses and directs events toward an end or resolution.

Plot as Design

The making of plots is a mimetic activity. We generally imagine that life is coherent and ordered and therefore look for the connections that will enable us to explain and understand the events we experience. Many events announce their significance and connection to other events. For example, a wedding elicits connections to events which precede and follow it. However, most of life's events do not announce their significance. Their connections with other events are not always apparent. Often an event's significance becomes clear only in retrospect, when there is an opportunity to evaluate its relation to other events. In order to discern meaning in events, we forge connections and discern coherent patterns.

It is not surprising, then, that our narratives also display this structuring activity and that we should demand a satisfying sense of coherence from them. Again following Ricoeur, the activity of making plots may be understood as a *poesis*, an imaginative process demonstrating both continuity and novelty. A plot unites a sequence of events into an apprehensible whole, establishing a logic by which the events may be understood and their significance appreciated. Plot offers a design through which the significance of each event can be appreciated by tracing its relationship to the whole.

Within a narrative, plot determines the manner in which each event is to be presented, what may be included and excluded, and how much attention each event may receive in proportion to the demands of its unfolding design. This shaping of the sequence of events is illustrated by the ways in which the Chronicler and the so-called Deuteronomist tell of the Israelite monarchy. While the Deuteronomist perceives Yahweh at work through significant events in both the northern and southern kingdoms, the Chronicler seems to see significance almost exclusively in the story of Judah. The deuteronomistic books of Samuel display a particular design in presenting David's story, including many unfavorable presentations of David. On the other hand, the Chronicler's narrative diligently expunges any negative references to David, and thus offers a far different portrait of his reign. The reigns of the remaining kings also receive different treatments by the Deuteronomist and the Chronicler. The Deuteronomist seems at points to employ a "bad king-good king" sequence, while the Chronicler presents both bad and good for each king who follows David. In each case, material is selected, presented, and ordered according to the pattern which the individual plot intends.

The nature of the connections and patterns which plot establishes between events should by now be clear. As we have discussed above, making connections between events is necessary in order to produce a plot. The primary (some would argue, the exclusive) means of connection is that of causality. Because Yahweh grants them victory, Israel is able to overcome the fortress of Jericho. Because Achan takes banned plunder, Israel is denied a victory at Ai. Because Israel purges itself of the offender and his family, the armies once again enjoy success against the peoples of the land.

Biblical plots are not, however, confined to strict causality in order to make the necessary linkages between events.[9] Repetition, for example, whether formal or thematic, broadens the context of a particular event so that its meaning can be appreciated in relation to patterns that may not be readily apparent. Such returns to an event draw both parallels and contrasts to past and future events.

Allusion, a particular form of repetition, brings a whole universe of meanings to a particular event by focusing through the lens of past or future. The account of Israel's crossing of the Jordan River in Joshua 3-5, for example, contains many allusions, implicit and explicit, to the Exodus and Sinai events. By connecting the present (Jordan) event with the past (Red Sea) event, the narrator expands the meaning of the Jordan crossing in its current context. The allusions also provide for the interweaving of a number of intersecting plot lines. The experiences of the present generation of Israelites, for instance, are linked to those of their parents and their ancestors. Joshua's plot in particular is enhanced and further intertwined with Israel's as he is cast, by word, deed, and description, in the image of Moses. The narrator is able to make these connections by thematic allusions to Sinai (the erection of twelve stones, the three days' wait, the call to consecration), by speeches (Joshua's connection of the crossings of the Red Sea and the Jordan) and by explicit commentary (the explanation for the circumcision at Gilgal).

In addition to causality, then, repetition of formal and thematic elements is a powerful connecting device within the book of Joshua.[10] Throughout the book, for example, the erection of stones or altars mark particularly meaningful events, events whose residue continues, as the narrator sometimes informs the reader, "to this day." Similarly, the language of oath and promise is reiterated throughout the book, forming an overarching pattern by which readers may understand and evaluate the events recounted.

Repetition also prompts the reader to reflect on the meaning of the connection as well as the meaning of the intervening events. The renewal of the covenant on Mount Ebal, following directly on Israel's experience at Ai, repeats the Sinai experience for the current generation of Israel. This renewal not only fulfills a previous commandment of Moses (Deut 27:1-8), but elicits a comparison of the contexts in which the two covenants have been enacted.

Finally, repetition ensures a "working out" of the plot so as to achieve a satisfactory resolution. The repetition of certain elements of the narrative indicates that those matters have not yet been put to rest. They await resolution and thus still "bear repeating."

Plot, then, unifies and configures events so that they can be followed. This sense of "followability" is vital, because the activity of making plots operates not only in the text but within the reader as well. The narrative text offers a particular configuration. The reader responds with interpretation. The confluence of the two activities is possible because, as we have discussed, both narrator and reader share certain conventions and perceptions—preunderstandings—regarding the nature of narrative. The reader's preunderstanding of the workings of narrative enables him or her to follow the pattern of events which the text presents. When interpreting a text the reader forms hypotheses based on the clues provided, renders a coherence by filling the gaps left in the story. Thus the interpreter derives a sense of the whole by which the narrative can be understood.

The preunderstandings held in common by both author and reader arise from human fictions of reality. The human tendency to render coherent and significant a perceived reality is concomitant with an expectation that narratives reflect that perceived order and wholeness. As Aristotle observed, a plot must therefore reflect this sense of order and coherence to some degree or it will not be satisfying. Expectations initiated at the beginning of a narrative must be satisfied, for we prefer fulfillment to disappointment.[11] These expectations of coherence and closure may, of course, be disregarded or flouted. But the uncomfortable sense that such operations create demonstrates the power of this impulse for concordance. Expectations of order and coherence extend to many areas of perception. Why, for example, do Mozart and Beethoven remain more popular than Bartok or Ives, if not, at least in part, because of a popular insistence that order prevail over discord?

The concord-making impulse prompts the reader to seek an explanation for the loose ends and mysteries that inhabit a narrative text. Our expectation of coherence is why, as Kermode observes, "we prefer enigmas to muddles" (Kermode 1979:53-54).

> Why, in fact, does it require a more strenuous effort to believe that a narrative lacks coherence than to believe that somehow, if we could only find out, it doesn't? . . . It is a prior expectation of consonance, the assumption that as readers we have to complete something capable of completion.

Kermode has convincingly demonstrated the power of the reader's desire for consonance, particularly in his exploration of the plethora of interpretations aroused by the notice of the "Boy in the Shirt" in the Gospel of Mark (Mark 14:51-52). He asks why interpreters have been attracted to the report, why they consistently perceive it as a puzzle which must have an explanation, and why all seem to ignore the possibility that it may have been included for no particular reason at all. We might ask the same questions of those who have sought to explain the report of Michal's barrenness (2 Sam 6:23). Why do interpreters, for the most part, assume some causal link between Michal's barrenness and her denigration of David, even though the text makes no such connection explicit? Here again, we encounter the desire for coherence. Why is it so difficult to regard Michal's childlessness as simply "a bitter coincidence, the last painful twist of a wronged woman's fate" (Alter 1983:125)?

Plot and Temporality

The orientation of events along a temporal grid gives the impression of time as an ordered sequence and thus satisfies the human impulse for coherence. Through plot, events are organized to give the sense of a beginning, middle, and end. Time is used to define and clarify events into an apprehensible whole. Temporal arrangement enables the reader to understand the connections and patterns by which disparate events are related. It marks particular events for special significance.

The organization of time as a way of creating an apprehensible whole is evident, for example, in the historian's development of plots for understanding historical phenomena in the ancient Near East. History is divided into sequential eras (the Bronze Age, Iron Age, etc.). Each of these "ages" is assigned a starting point and terminus, as any time-line or chart demonstrates. The designations provide a framework in which connections between a wide variety of historical phenomena can be apprehended. For example, the end of the Bronze Age is commonly fixed at 1200 BCE, a date that also marks the beginning of the Iron Age. The date corresponds roughly to the collapse of ancient cultures and their replacement by new ones. However, no one believes that, suddenly in the year 1200 BCE, everyone threw down their bronze implements and started using iron, or that the Sea Peoples made a mad dash for the eastern Mediterranean as if in response to some cosmic starter's pistol. The circumstances of that time period were undoubtedly more complex and fluid. Yet the demarcation is useful. If we were to ask a historian the question "What happened during the Iron Age?" we would probably receive a more or less coherent narrative in response.

In the process of making concords, certain events in time become endowed with particular meaning. By investing certain events with significance, a concept of time is adopted that supersedes the reality of time as a mere sequence of events. The construction of plots therefore produces an "escape from chronicity," enabling the maintenance of the belief that events have meaning. The experience of time as *chronos*, reality as a simple sequence, thus is disputed and repressed by the perception of time as a pattern of *kairoi*. This is particularly true with respect to mythic or sacred concepts of time, which confer special significance to such things as new moons or rituals. In ancient Babylon, for instance, the concord-maker Marduk sallied forth each Fall during the New Year's Festival to overcome the monstrous forces of chaos. So also, after seven days of following the Ark around the city of Jericho, the people shout, watch the disintegration of the city, and destroy its inhabitants.

Plot, then, might be considered "an organization that humanizes time by giving it form" (Kermode 1979:45). This organizing impulse can be seen clearly in the book of Joshua. The book is framed by the reports of two sets of deaths: the death of Moses (1:2) at the beginning, and those of Joshua and Eleazar (24:28-29,33) at the conclusion. Significant events, moreover, such as the crossing of the Jordan, are marked by relatively long presentations and by allusions which interpret the present event through recollection of past experiences and promises. Further, connections are made between past, present, and future as Israel's victories and covenants are commemorated by the erection of altars or monoliths, some of which, we read, are standing "to this day" (4:9; 5:9; 6:25; 7:26; 8:29; etc.). Conventions of temporal organization are also manipulated by the text in regard to the acquisition of the land: a promise at the brink of fulfillment at the beginning of the book (1:2-5), a *fait accompli* at points in between (12:7-24; 21:43-45), and a promise yet to be realized at the end (23:4-5).

A wide variety of devices may be employed to transform the story sequence into a narrative. These have been codified most extensively by Gerard Genette (1980), who divides the artifices of temporal presentation into three categories: order, duration, and frequency. First, Genette calls attention to the distinction between the sequence of events as presented in the narrative (*récit*, narrative time) and the actual sequence of the story events (*histoire*, story time) and examines the ways by which narratives manipulate the chronological order of a story. In order to forge connections between events, the narrative may evoke an event that takes place later (prolepsis) or earlier (analepsis) than the given textual moment. Both devices are used effectively in the speeches which begin and end the book of Joshua. Analeptic narrations at the beginning recall the words of Moses, while those at the end rehearse Yahweh's deeds on Israel's behalf, from the time of Abraham onward. Proleptic elements in the beginning discourse articulate the potential for blessing and fulfillment in the land, while those at the end intimate Israel's eventual expulsion.

Second, the duration of events presented in the narrative may also be regulated. One series of events may be cursorily summarized, while other events may take on a "scenic" quality, so that the time of presenting correlates more closely with "real time." Through such a device the importance of events to the design of the plot can be indicated. In Joshua, a significant portion of text time is devoted to the initial conquests of Jericho and Ai, while later campaigns (those in the south and north) are summarized briefly. The elaboration of city and boundary lists during the tribal assemblies gives them a scenic quality, as if the listing of each town and village in the text mirrors its assignment to a tribe or group during the actual assembly. By noting the events to which the plot devotes a significant body of text, the reader may gain a better sense of the importance of those events to the development of the plot.

Genette's third category, frequency, deals with the relationship between an event or series of events, and the number of times those events may be related in the text. The variations range from narrating one event many times to recounting once something that happened many times. In Joshua, specific events generally are related only once. However, when events are repeated, they may lend significance to the new situation. When the Israelites in Canaan accuse the eastern tribes of disobedience, for example, they remind them of the consequences of Achan's sin. The repetition of Achan's sin thereby carries an implicit threat: the circumstances are similar, and what happened before may happen again.

The Sense of an Ending

As one reads a narrative text, the events recounted assume a design that points to a resolution. Thus we speak of a plot developing or unfolding. The organization of events into coherent configurations implies a beginning and end which render the open-endedness of time into a manageable whole. Again, it is Kermode who, in his examination of apocalyptic thinking, focuses attention on the human impulse to seek coherence through intelligible ends (1966:17):

> Men in the middest make considerable imaginative investments in coherent patterns which, by the provision of an end, make possible a satisfying consonance with the origins and with the middle.

Ends promise fulfillment; they complete the design and make possible apprehension of the whole. Only when the end has been reached, and all the pieces have been fitted, can the full meaning of the whole be understood. We therefore expect ends to reinforce our fictions of concordance and to provide a clarification and interpretation of the pattern of events.

The end provides a destination for the configuration of events, a goal toward which the plot is directed. This movement toward the end gives plot its dynamic quality. Events are shaped into a pattern, and obstacles which threaten alternative and unsatisfactory endings are overcome so that the desired sense of closure may be achieved. The desire for consonance corresponds to a desire for intelligible ends, ends that "make sense" and reinforce the constructs by which life is integrated and invested with meaning. Plausible ends are those which satisfy the assumptions that all events can be connected to others and that everything can somehow be explained.

PLOTS AND OBSCURITY

To an extent, all narratives exhibit some element of obscurity. Even though plots commonly present patterns of coherence, they also raise questions and tensions, and often seem to hinder interpretation and comprehension. The passage with which we began this chapter is a good example. In the brief account of Joshua and the commander of Yahweh's army, we encounter an episode that is both affirming and menacing. Why do narratives, which present themselves as expressions of concordance, contain elements that tend to obscure?

One reason is pragmatic. Tension and suspense are essential for capturing and holding a reader's interest. Tension is created by intimating the possibility of unexpected or unwanted endings. This makes the fulfillment of expectation uncertain and increases the reader's involvement as the story nears a resolution. Will Israel succeed in taking possession of the promised land? Will Yahweh remain with Israel?

On another level, the answer may be found in the nature of narrative's representation of reality. Although desires for concordance are deeply rooted, a plot that is too perfectly contrived may be rejected, because the reader knows that connections are not always easily made and coherence is not easily detected. A reader may therefore reject concords that are too easily made and conclusions that are too neatly drawn.[12] A certain element of obscurity is thus essential for making and interpreting plots. The feints and detours, the obstacles and indeterminacies which are a part of a plot, mirror our experience of a world in which answers and meaning are rarely explicit. The meanings of our own stories often lie in secrecy, and the unraveling of alternative—past, present, and future—is a difficult and uncertain business.

Turning to biblical narrative, one encounters relatively coherent plots in such books as Ruth and Genesis, which can be followed without much effort. In these narratives the obstacles to a satisfying end are effectively overcome. On the other hand, the book of Joshua renders powerful obstructions which challenge the promise of fulfillment and threaten hopes for a satisfactory conclusion. Its images of plenitude and concordance are countered throughout the text by representations of failure and fragmentation. And while it offers a formal closure, it leaves much of the story in suspension. By the time the book reaches its conclusion, Israel has been disintegrated (permanently, it seems), not only by the presence of banned peoples in its midst, but also by the rift caused by tribes who do not wish to accept an inheritance in the holy land. "Outsiders" who are now in and "insiders" who are now out all join with the assembled multitude at Shechem. Large enclaves of Canaanites, furthermore, remain interspersed among the Israelites. Even the covenant made and renewed with the One God is fractured by the intimations of disobedience and the presence of other gods among the people.

PLOT AND DESIRE

The correspondence between the mind's structuring activity and the plotting of narratives has recently been explored by Peter Brooks. Brooks calls attention to the psychic processes involved in the production and interpretation of literature; composition and reading are but two manifestations of the mind's structuring activity (1987:4). He writes,

> The structure of literature is in some sense the structure of mind—not a specific mind, but . . . "the mental apparatus," which is more accurately the dynamic organization of the psyche, a process of structuration. We continue to dream of a convergence of psychoanalysis and literary criticism because we sense that there ought to be, that there must be, some correspondence between literary and psychic process, that aesthetic structure and form, including literary tropes, must somehow coincide with the psychic structures and operations they both evoke and appeal to.

Assuming this connection between psychic and textual functioning, Brooks derives a model of plot from the Freudian masterplot for biological life. His model is attuned not only to literary devices, rhetorical structures and textual strategies, but also to the investment of these structures with desire and force. The literary text may therefore be perceived as a "system of internal energies and tensions, compulsions, resistances, and desires" (1984:xiv).

The initial arousal of desire at the beginning of a narrative, usually a state of sufficient intensity as to require movement, action, or change, marks its "coming to life"—its stimulation from quiescence into narratability. The goal of the ensuing narration is the satisfaction to be gained in the release of this tension and in a return to quiescence. Described in these terms, the operation of plot is analogous to Freud's description of biological desire; the desire for satisfaction corresponds to the notion of a "pleasure principle," while the drive toward the end may be seen to correspond with the "death instinct." Just as the death instinct drives an organism to seek a "death in its own way," so a narrative is driven toward a desired ending— one that will bring a sense of fulfillment, closure, and satisfaction.[13]

The desired end promises an illumination of the meaning of the story, but this end must be delayed so that it can be understood in relation to the beginning. This delay, which is the "middle" of a narrative, is accomplished through a constant process of repetition. By repeating certain themes and motifs, the threats of premature or undesired endings are worked through and mastered, much as Freud saw in a child's *fort-da* game an attempt to master his mother's absence. Repetition in literary narratives, suggests Brooks, represents a suspension of the temporal process, a return to a prior event. The middle of the narrative can therefore be perceived as a detour or deviance—a movement from passivity to mastery—as obstacles and potentially undesired endings are worked through and a sense of fulfillment is eventually achieved.

The energies and desires Brooks describes are not resident in the actual paper and ink of the literary text but rather are activated when it is read; that is, when a reader enters into discourse with the text. Implicit in a narrative text is an impulse to tell, an urge to implicate the reader in the playing out of desire. By entering into dialogue with the text, the reader therefore brings about the animation of those desires which underlie the narration.[14]

The interpretive work of the reader is also invested with desire. The reader desires fulfillment as well. In entering the fictive system presented by the text, the reader works to make sense of it and to master its energies, rewriting and reshaping the story, and making it accessible to his or her own needs. Here again, Brooks perceives an analogy: the dialogue between text and reader is much like that between analysand and analyst. Like the analyst, the reader of a literary text undertakes an activity of radical construction. He or she constantly intervenes in the story being told, listening carefully to discern connections and patterns, creating hypotheses, and seeking ultimately a more coherent rendering of it. Like the analyst, the reader seeks the "totality of the supreme." In the process, hypotheses are continuously put to the text for verification. The process of interpretation thus leads to the evolution of the story as it is shaped and rewritten by the reader, whose perceptions are likewise shaped and reformed by the text. Thus, while one may recognize a transference of desire from the text to the reader, a counter-transferential desire can be detected in the reader as well, as he or she seeks to master the text and to be mastered by it.[15] Meaning, according to this model, is therefore located not in the author, text, or reader, but in the "artificial space" created by the act of reading.

The psychoanalytic model offers a number of insights that will be useful for our analysis of plot in Joshua. First, the model acknowledges the connection between plot and the configuring activity of the mind; literary form has a dynamic quality that is activated during the reading process. Second, this approach calls attention more explicitly to the place of desire in the production of plots, and thus explains the desires for coherence, fulfillment, and closure that are present in the exchange between text and reader. Finally, the importance of repetition is emphasized. More than merely one technique in a catalogue of rhetorical devices, repetition can be conceived as a primary operation of plot and a significant manifestation of desire.

PLOT AND THE BOOK OF JOSHUA

We shall employ this notion of desire as a primary metaphor for understanding the operation of plot in Joshua. Desire addresses the initiation of plot, the kinds of endings to which plot moves, and the patterns which connect beginning to end. In a sense, Israel's larger story, of which Joshua is but one segment, comes to life with the movement of Abraham from a static condition to an active state (Gen 12:1ff). Expectation and promise are present at this beginning as desire is manifested in the promise of a land. The land promise is repeated continuously throughout the books of the Pentateuch until it reaches the brink of fulfillment just as the book of Joshua begins. The force of this desire, its fulfillment long-postponed by various detours, is such that only one ending can give a sense of satisfaction—Israel in possession of Canaan.

Yahweh's promise to give Israel the land of Canaan may therefore be viewed as a manifestation of textual desire. This desire is restated at the very outset of Joshua, but it is accompanied by the appearance of resistances that threaten to derail the movement of the plot toward its expected fulfillment. Joshua must be exhorted by both God and people. Joshua's rejoinder to the Reubenites, Gadites, and the half-tribe of Manasseh bespeaks an Israel already fractured. The presence of both fulfillment and unfulfillment at the beginning of Joshua demonstrates a tension that constitutes the principle dynamic of the story.

In reading Joshua, we shall be concerned with two fundamental questions. First, what form does desire assume? And second, how does desire shape the contours of its plots? In order to answer these questions, we will mark the following: explicit commentary on the story, repetition of motifs and key terms, the presentation and resolution of the disruptive aspects of the story, and the way the story is brought to a close.

Commentary and summaries of events, whether given by the narrator or a character within the story, establish patterns of coherence by linking and interpreting the events of the story. These devices therefore appear as the most obvious signs of plot. In particular, we will be concerned to note how the narrator's interpretation of events corresponds to, or contrasts with, the events as they are narrated.

Repeated motifs, symbols, and structural patterns will receive special attention. In Joshua, repeated disruptions appear in the form of Israelite disobedience to Yahweh and failure to secure the entire land. These disruptions are, in turn, repeatedly countered by presentations of Israelite fidelity and success. The patterns created by the interplay of these repetitions form the dynamic by which the story is directed toward its conclusion.

Marking the disruptive aspects of the story will also be important in tracing plot. We will note particularly how disruptions, such as the episode of the Gibeonite covenant and the reports of land not taken, are presented and resolved. Does the banishment of Rahab from the camp completely resolve the problem of her presence within Israel, or are the tensions created by the episode glossed and repressed?

Finally, the importance of endings demands that we devote special attention to the concluding section of Joshua (chapters 22 through 24). Joshua seems to "end" a number of times. The story of the altar at Geliloth, Joshua's "farewell address," and the covenant ceremony at Shechem all concern questions of obedience, integrity, and fulfillment. How does the ending presented correspond to the end expected? Does the ending bring a sense of completion and closure? Has a resolution of the major tensions ben achieved?

In bringing this chapter to a close, we may apply our reading strategy to the episode with which we began: the uncanny story of the commander of the army. The episode occurs immediately after Israel has affirmed its obedience to Yahweh through the ritual of circumcision and the celebration of the Passover, and it immediately precedes the siege of Jericho. The commander's appearance therefore elicits a desire to affirm Yahweh's favor. However, the commander's sword is unsheathed, and he stands in Joshua's way. Angels with swords are associated with punishment and warnings. The apparition is therefore menacing as well, hinting that Israel has warranted punishment by some act of disobedience. The commander leaves Joshua's question open. Is Yahweh for or against Israel?

3

CONQUEST
AND
COMPROMISE

Subjugation of the land of Canaan by the Israelites is the topic of the first major section of Joshua (chapters 1-12). Capping the account, Israel's military exploits are recapitulated in a sequence of summaries that moves from specific to general: victories in northern Canaan (11:12-15), conquests west of the Jordan (11:16-23), and all Israelite conquests, both east and west of the Jordan (12:1-24).

The first two summaries offer explicit evaluations based on one of two primary concerns. The first (11:12-15) evaluates Israel's conduct regarding the peoples of the land and asserts its *obedience* to the law of Moses (vss. 12b, 15). The second (11: 16-23) affirms the totality of conquest, demonstrating a concern for *integrity* (vss. 16-17, 23). These summaries also display similar formats. Each begins with a positive assertion, opposes the assertion with conflicting information, and concludes with a reaffirmation of the opening statement. Thus, the middle of each text is at variance with its beginning and end.

These two summary texts exhibit, in miniature, the configurational agenda which characterizes the entire book. The obedience and integrity of Israel constitute the two primary trajectories for the story related in Joshua. And while Joshua begins and ends with strong affirmations of these motifs, its middle contains information which contradicts these affirmations. Taken as paradigms for the whole, a close reading of these two texts will provide an introduction to the dynamic operation of plot in Joshua.

ALL THAT YAHWEH COMMANDED

The summary of the northern campaign (11:12-15) begins and ends with the narrator affirming Joshua's complete obedience to the commandments of Yahweh and Moses. These comments form an *inclusio* (a repetition which marks off the enclosed text) encouraging the reader to view the intervening material in the light of Moses' commandments, particularly those elements that deal with the conquest of cities and the application of the ban. The *inclusio* emphatically affirms Joshua's (and, by extension, Israel's) complete obedience to the law of Moses. However, the intervening material seems to contradict these assertions.

> All the cities of these kings, as well as the kings themselves, Joshua captured, and he struck them with the edge of the sword. He put them under the ban just as Moses the servant of Yahweh had commanded.
>
> However, Israel did not burn any of the cities located on tels, with the exception of Hazor. It was the only one Joshua burned. And all the plunder and livestock of these cities the Israelites seized for themselves. However, the people they struck with the edge of the sword until they had annihilated them. Nothing that breathed remained.
>
> As Yahweh commanded Moses his servant, so Moses commanded Joshua, and so Joshua did. He did not stray from anything that Yahweh had commanded Moses. (11:12-15)

Something seems amiss. The beginning and concluding assertions are emphatically stated, but the intervening material presents a chain of exceptions and qualifications. The Hebrew particle *raq*, which signals a qualification or limitation ("except," "only"),[1] is used effectively here to bring the exceptions into sharp relief. First, only Hazor is actually destroyed (What of the other great cities of the region, such as Megiddo or Beth-Shean?). Second, the application of the ban at Hazor is less than rigorous. The ban, in fact, is selectively applied; livestock and booty are taken from the cities, even though all the people are killed. The repeated assertions of fidelity to the commandments of Moses raise important questions as well. What *did* Moses say about the conquest and disposition of Canaanite cities and their inhabitants? Has the ban been applied appropriately? Are these reports consistent with Moses' directives?

Regarding the disposition of the inhabitants of Canaan, the Mosaic law is unambiguous. Israel is to exterminate the indigenous inhabitants, so that "nothing that breathes" will remain (Deut 20:16; cf. Exod 23:33; Deut 7:2, 24). The Canaanites represent a threat to the covenant with Yahweh, and Israel is prohibited from making any kind of agreement or treaty with them. Failure to execute the commandment therefore brings serious consequences. If allowed to remain in the land the indigenous inhabitants will lead Israel away from Yahweh, and then Yahweh will "do to you what I plan to do to them" (Num 33:56; cf. Exod 23:32; Deut 7:2-4, 25-26; 12:29-31).

Turning to the Mosaic directives for warfare and the application of the ban in Deut 20:1-20, one encounters two sets of rules. The first addresses warfare in general, waged against cities "at a distance" (vss. 10-15). In this case, the people of the city may be given an opportunity to surrender, and if they accept, Israel may subject them to servitude. If they refuse to surrender, Israel is still permitted to carry off the booty, plunder, women, and children (the restrictions here being marked by the adverb *raq*; vs. 14). Only the men of the city must be killed.

The second scenario concerns warfare against the inhabitants of Canaan (vss. 16-18). In this case, Israel must slay "everything that breathes," and must place the city under the ban. These stipulations presuppose others previously given ("as Yahweh your God has commanded you"; vs. 17b), evidently referring to earlier instructions for the application of the ban in Deuteronomy 7. Moses' words in Deut 20:16-18 are therefore reinforced by the commandments given in Deut 7: Israel must put all Canaan's inhabitants under the ban (7:1-2), destroy altars and idols (7:5-6, 25a), and respect the ban regarding the booty (7:25b-26).

The words of Moses make it clear that livestock, booty, and captives may be taken from a conquered city, except when that conquered city is within the land of promise. In such a case, that city is to be placed under the ban, and no living thing is to be spared. Viewed from this perspective, it appears that Israel's activity, reported in Josh 11:13-14, is in clear violation of the commandments set forth by Moses. Joshua is correct in applying the ban to the northern Canaanite cities, but the disposition of the plunder is undertaken as if these cities were non-Canaanite and therefore not subject to the ban. How can the narrator say, then, that Joshua "did not stray from anything that Yahweh had commanded Moses?"

The tension raised by this text is serious. Israel's obedience is essential to achieving a satisfactory conclusion for the story, for Moses decrees that Israel will succeed in taking possession of the promised land only if it is completely obedient to Yahweh's commandments (Exod 23:20-31; Deut 6:18-19; 8:1; 11:8-9, 18-21, 31-32). Conversely, rebellion and disobedience on the part of Israel will result in any number of very unsatisfactory conclusions: failure, disintegration, and destruction (Exod 23:32-33; Num 33:55-56; Deut 11:26-28; 28:15ff). Moses' law concerning Israel's conduct in the land follows a simple logic. If the Israelites are obedient, Yahweh will enable them to take possession of Canaan. If they are not obedient, Yahweh will turn against them and they will not be able to live in the land. The intervening material in 11:13-14 therefore represents a threat to the desired ending intimated by the opening and closing affirmations.

Readers have dealt with this inconsistency between evaluation and report in a variety of ways. The most common approach is to take the evaluative remarks at face value and gloss the tension. Thus, for example, "God's perfect leader chose to follow God's perfect command and thus reap God's perfect victory" (Butler 1983:129). Other interpreters suggest that the narrator is giving a true and reliable evaluation of events, but, for a variety of reasons, the reader is not completely acquainted with the conventions appropriated by the narrator. Perhaps there were recognized conditions under which the ban could be annulled or set aside.[2]

Robert Polzin refines the latter perspective, arguing that the tension in the passage is the result of two differing *interpreta-*

tions of the words of Moses: a strict and inflexible application of the commandments versus a more expansive and merciful approach. The narrator is aligned with the latter perspective and is therefore inclined to exaggerate. The excepted material belongs to a more irenic perspective, which argues here, as throughout Joshua, that as the excepted people of the land have been shown mercy, so God has shown mercy to an Israel which, in light of a strict application of Moses' words, has not deserved it.[3]

We may well ask, however, if Moses' words will stretch so far. The rigid form of the commandments seems to allow little room for interpretation. The material related in verses 13-14 represents a violation of the commandments regarding the people of the land and thus stands in direct opposition to the assertions of obedience in verses 12 and 15.

The summary of 11:12-15 manifests a desire to tell Israel's story in terms of obedience to Moses and Yahweh: Joshua "put them under the ban, just as Moses the servant of Yahweh had commanded." This desire is opposed, however, by the claims that Israel burned only one city and took plunder from cities under the ban. These exceptions challenge the affirmation of an obedient Israel and must be resolved so that a sense of satisfaction can be achieved. A dynamic is therefore created by the struggle to master the resistance of the disruptive information, which is subsequently met with an emphatic response: "As Yahweh commanded Moses his servant, so Moses commanded Joshua, and so Joshua did. He did not stray from any word which Yahweh commanded Moses" (vs. 15). The threatening image of disobedience is countered and bound by rigorous and repeated assertions that all was done in obedience to the commands of Moses. The text therefore works in complicity with the reader's desire for closure and represses the threat to a proper ending.

JOSHUA TOOK THE ENTIRE LAND

The summary of Israel's victories in northern Canaan (11:12-15) is followed by another more expansive summary of the conquests of Joshua and Israel throughout the land (11:16-23). Like the previous summary, 11:16-23 is framed by strong and unequivocal affirmations. However, in this case the summary manifests a desire to affirm Israel's integrity rather than its obedience. The narrator begins and ends with the assertion that "Joshua took the entire land" (vss. 16, 23), but (as in 11:12-15) places material in between which undercuts this assertion.

> Joshua took this entire land: the hill country, the entire Negeb, the entire land of Goshen, the Shephelah, the Arabah, the hill country of Israel and the foothills—from Mount Halak upwards towards Seir, as far as Baal-Gad in the Valley of Lebanon below Mount Hermon. All their kings he captured. He struck them and put them to death.
>
> For many years Joshua waged war against all these kings. There was not a city which made peace with the Israelites, with the exception of the Hivite inhabitants of Gibeon. He took everything in battle, because it was from Yahweh to harden their hearts to engage Israel in battle so that he might put them under the ban so as to show them no mercy; so that he might annihilate them as Yahweh commanded Moses.
>
> Joshua proceeded at that time to cut off the Anakim from the hill country; from Hebron, Debir, Anab, from the entire hill country of Judah, and from the entire hill country of Israel. Along with their cities, Joshua put them under the ban. None of the Anakim remained within the land of Israel. However, there were some left in Gaza, Gath and Ashdod.
>
> Joshua took the entire land, according to everything that Yahweh had spoken to Moses. And Joshua gave it to Israel as an inheritance, according to their portions as tribes. The land rested from battle. (11:16-23)

The opening and closing sections of the passage emphatically assert that Joshua "took the entire land." The opening assertion is reinforced by a description of the extent of land successfully taken and the kings successfully defeated (vss. 16-17). Likewise, the closing assertion affirms Israel's ultimate victory in the land by looking proleptically toward the allotment of territory to the tribes and reporting the cessation of military activity (vs. 23).

Between these unequivocal pronouncements, however, the reader encounters a good deal of ambiguity. The material can be subdivided into two sections. The first (vss. 18-20) summarizes Joshua's campaigns in Canaan, while the second (vss. 21-22) relates his successes against the Anakim. Each section contains information which opposes the narrator's claim of complete success, just as the material in 11:13-14 opposed the narrator's claim that Joshua had acted in complete obedience to the words of Moses (11:12,15).

The first section contains three pieces of information: 1) the warfare between Israel and the land's inhabitants raged for a long period of time, 2) the cities of the land made no peace with Israel and were taken—with the exception of Gibeon, and 3) Yahweh had hardened the hearts of the people of the land so that Israel could exterminate them. Each of these data weakens the narrator's claim of a comprehensive victory in Canaan. The first is an admission that, despite the impression of comprehensive victory reported in 10:1-43 and 11:1-15, the business of subjugating the land's inhabitants was protracted and (we may therefore assume) not easily accomplished.

The second piece of information offers a more direct challenge. Despite the claims that all cities were taken in battle, there is one exception. Gibeon's appearance fractures the holistic tone of the summary, positing a significant and troubling dissent.

Finally, the narrator states that Yahweh had hardened the hearts of the inhabitants of the land to engage Israel in battle. On the surface, this appears to reinforce the claim of Israel's comprehensive success: Yahweh intervened on Israel's behalf so that the inhabitants of the land could be annihilated. However, the declaration also raises certain questions. Why is it necessary for Yahweh to impel the land's inhabitants to take the initiative against Israel, so that Israel is forced into confrontations with the people they are to exterminate? Has Israel's zeal dissipated? Such questions are encouraged by the redundant chain of purpose clauses which explains Yahweh's reason for hardening the hearts: "to engage (*liqra't*) Israel in battle so that (*lema'an*) he might put them under the ban so as to (*lebilti*) show them no mercy; so that (*lema'an*) he might annihilate them" (v. 20b). Israel's mission, it is repeatedly affirmed, is to destroy the nations of Canaan, and Yahweh, by causing the Canaanites to initiate battle, must act to ensure this.[4]

Yahweh has thus been at work among the inhabitants of the land, so that they do not make peace with Israel. This comment, immediately following the mention of Gibeon, raises further questions. If Yahweh has indeed been hardening the hearts of the land's inhabitants, why does Yahweh not harden the hearts of the Gibeonites as well? Why does Yahweh allow them to "make peace" with the Israelites (9:6, 11, 15)?[5]

The second section (11:21-22) details Joshua's exploits against the Anakim, who are driven from a number of cities as well as the hill country. Once again the reader is confronted with an assertion immediately undercut by an exception: "None of the Anakim remained within the land of Israel. However, (*raq*) there were some left in Gaza, Gath and Ashdod" (v. 22). At first glance the report seems straightforward enough; Joshua succeeded in driving the Anakim out of the land claimed by Israel. Yet the particle *raq* signals the reader that the information to follow qualifies that given previously. The report that no Anakim remained in Israel, except in Gaza, Gath, and Ashdod, gives the impression that these three cities lie within the land Israel is to take.

Indeed, the region comprising Gaza, Gath, and Ashdod does fall within the general assignment of land given to Israel (1:4; cf. Num 34:1-12) and will later be assigned by lot to Judah (15:45-47).[6] The note is a tacit admission that Joshua did not actually take the entire land promised to Israel, and it therefore contests the assertion of a comprehensive Israelite victory. Not only a city, but an entire region has escaped Joshua's sword. Again the contradiction is clear. Given these significant exceptions, how can it be affirmed that the entire land was taken?

As in the previous text, the tension is marked. The land represents, above all, an ordered and defined existence—a life without deficiency. It therefore signifies satisfaction, offering the promise of "a special kind of life—good, undefiled, life in community, life in the worship of Yahweh, life at its fullest and best" (P. Miller 1969:458).[7] Its possession assumes an identification of land with people, and therefore expresses a desire for homogeneity. For Israel, possession of the land ensures integrity.[8]

Desire for the land reflects a desire for integrity. This understanding is reinforced by the Mosaic form of the Land Promise. In Deuteronomy, the book which immediately precedes Joshua, the promise of the land is rendered as an imperative; "go in and take possession of the land" (Deut 1:39; 4:1; 5:31; 12:1; 15:4; 17:4; 19:2, 14; 25:19; 26:1).[9] The book of Joshua begins with a repeated exhortation, first to Joshua and then to Israel, to "take possession" of the land promised by Yahweh (1:2-5; 10-11). The promise of the land, rendered in the form of a command, emphasizes the conditional nature of the promise; the promise will only be fulfilled by an energetic response on Israel's part. Yahweh gives the land; Israel must take possession of it.

The law of Moses unequivocally predicts that fulfillment will remain elusive if the conditions are not met, that is, if that which is "not-Israel" remains in the land (Exod 23:33; 34:15-16; Num 33:55-56; Deut 7:4; 12:29-31). The disruptive reports in Josh 11:18-22 thus threaten the promise of satisfaction offered in the assertions that Joshua took the entire land. This disruption must be mastered so that a sense of fulfillment can be achieved.

The dynamic detected in 11:12-15 is therefore at work in 11:16-23 as well. Both passages are framed by unqualified affirmations. Yet each contains material which challenges the organizing pattern asserted by its beginning and concluding declarations. In the case of 11:16-23, the primary motif is not obedience but integrity. The tension here is between a desire to depict Israel's complete success on the one hand, and disruptive information which reports significant failures on the other.

The working out of this dynamic is marked by certain repeated symbols and motifs. Desire is manifested by repeated assertions that Israel has been entirely successful; all Goshen and the Negeb (vs. 16), all the hill country (vs. 21), and, indeed, the whole land (vss. 16, 23) was taken. All the kings were defeated (vss. 17,18) and all the cities were taken (v. 19). The Hebrew term *kol*, signifying wholeness and totality, is repeated nine times within this passage, its frequent repetition under-scoring the sense of comprehensive victory.[10] The sense of totality is also reinforced by the claim that Yahweh was working on Israel's behalf to bring about the divinely ordained destruction.

On the other hand, dissonant patterns of fragmentation and failure are evident in the repeated appearance of "exceptions" (introduced by *bilti* and *raq*) and the notes about remaining peoples and regions. The interplay of plots in this section can be conceived as a contest. The claim of total victory is introduced and elaborated (vss. 16-17), then countered by the excepting data (vss. 18-19), and subsequently reaffirmed by a claim of divine intervention (vs. 20). The claim of victory is made again on a regional level in verse 21, but is again opposed by the significant exceptions listed in verse 22. This opposition in turn leads to the emphatic reassertion of the introductory declaration (vs. 23), which is given a sense of finality by a proleptic account of the next phase of the story.

THE CONTEST OF PLOTS IN JOSHUA

The desire manifested by these summary passages (for obedience and integrity), as well as the tensions and contradictions they raise, are characteristic of the entire book. The text of Joshua consistently juxtaposes episodes that illustrate Israel's obedience to Yahweh with others that tell of the disobedience. The successful victories at Jericho, Ai, and Gibeon, for example, are all related in detail, but connected with each campaign is a story which tells of an incident that violates the Mosaic commandments. Each of these disruptive stories appears immediately after Israel's obedience has been presented or affirmed. In similar fashion, the reader encounters a tendency to structure the narrative in terms of wholes: Israel takes all the land, Israel acts as one people, the land is ordered into homogenous units, and Yahweh acts in complete concord with Israel. However, significant portions of the text oppose this construct: large areas of land remain to be taken, Israel cannot drive out the inhabitants, boundaries are blurred, and Yahweh is not always with Israel.

The desire to affirm obedience and integrity links the events of the story and orients them toward a satisfactory end. On the other hand, dissonant aspects of the story, expressed as disobedience and the fragmentation of Israel and its land, oppose the structures of desire and orient the story toward an undesirable end (failure and a threatened expulsion). These patterns of desire and dissonance may be regarded as plots.

The two plots which determine the ostensible configuration of the story, orienting it in the direction of fulfillment, we will call *ostensive plots*. The first ostensive plot, of obedience, is advanced by repeated references to and portrayals of Israel's fidelity. The second, a plot of integrity, characterized by the casting of events in comprehensive and holistic terms, can be discerned in the ubiquitous depictions of a united Israel which successfully possesses the promised land.

The two dissonant patterns which oppose the movement toward fulfillment may be referred to as *opposing plots*. The first, a disruptive plot of disobedience, counters the representation of Israelite obedience with episodes which present violations of Yahweh's commandments. The second, a plot of fragmentation, opposes the sense of Israelite integrity with presentations of Israelite disunity and failure.

The dynamic created by the interaction of ostensive and opposing plots is a struggle to gain mastery over textual dissonances so that concordance may be established and the desired end achieved. The ostensive and opposing plots create a network of competing patterns, pitting disappointment against fulfillment, dissatisfaction against satisfaction, and indeterminacy against closure. Interacting, these plots create a dynamic that drives the narrative to its conclusion, while rendering uncertain the fulfillment of the land promise.

This contest is evident in certain repeated symbols and motifs. Marking the ostensive plot line of obedience, the primary configuration of Joshua 1-12, are frequent references to the proper execution of Yahweh's commandments through Moses and Joshua (the root *tsawah*, "command," occurs 31 times in this section) and to the performance of various religious rituals (3:5-4:24; 5:2-12; 6:1ff; 7:13-26; 8:30-35; 18:1-10; 24:1ff).

Through repeated episodes portraying Israel's fidelity to the commandments and its concern for proper religious observance, the plot of obedience expands and develops.

The opposing plot of disobedience, which pushes the narrative in the direction of failure, can be discerned in incidents which depict infractions of the law of Moses. The promise of the land is threatened by swearing forbidden oaths and taking forbidden plunder. Israel's covenant relationship with Yahweh, moreover, is threatened by covenants with the people of the land. The repeated motifs of swearing oaths, making covenants, and executing the ban thus mark in Joshua the patterns of dissonance which counter the drive toward fulfillment.

The desire for integration is apparent in the tendency to present the action of the narrative in terms of wholes and units, and is most often signified by the use of the inclusive term *kol.* References to "all Israel" (1:2; 3:1; 5:5; 8:15, 21; 10:29; 24:1) and "the entire congregation" (9:18; 18:1; 22:18) are frequent, and Israel's subjugation of the land is itself rendered in comprehensive terms (11:16, 23; 12:9-24). Furthermore, the allotment of land to the tribes expresses a sense of order and completion.

On the other hand, repeated instances of Israel's failure to eliminate the peoples of Canaan (i.e., Rahab, the Gibeonites, the cities on tels) and intimations that Yahweh is not always "with" Israel (7:1ff) disrupt the construct of total victory rendered in chapters 1-12. These disruptions become more pronounced in chapters 13-21, where the desire for possession becomes the dominant configurational agenda. Here we discover numerous accounts of failure to dispossess the inhabitants of the land, as well as reports of territory not taken (13:1-5, 13; 15:63; 16:10; 17:12-13; 19:47-48), both of which fragment the finely-drawn lines of tribal integrity.

The tension between plots creates a dynamic which moves the narrative from the other side of the Jordan to Israel's apparent subjugation of the promised land. Promises are made by Israel that counter the promise made to Israel, boundaries of various types are blurred and abolished, and the closure offered at the end cannot overcome the traces of another, more ominous, end yet to come. The opposing energies which these patterns and motifs signify repeatedly disrupt the movement toward concordance and satisfaction, constantly threatening a premature and unsatisfactory end. In turn, these resistances are answered by affirmations that redirect the story towards fulfillment. The operation of these plots leaves the ending in suspense. Will the Israelites' transgressions cause Yahweh to make an end to them? Will Israel gain the land?

4

OBEDIENCE
AND
DISOBEDIENCE

INITIAL EXHORTATIONS

B eginning the book of Joshua is a series of speeches: Yahweh to Joshua (vss. 1-9), Joshua to the Israelite officials
(vss. 10-11), Joshua to the eastern tribes (vss. 12-15), and the
eastern tribes to Joshua (vss. 16-18). We meet little original
material: the speeches patch together various bits and pieces of
material drawn from Deuteronomy. Beginning this way emphasizes the importance of the Mosaic commandments for the plots
of the book of Joshua and encourages the reader to begin con-
structing the story in terms of the issues and concerns articulated by Moses.

Yahweh's speech (vss. 1-9) reminds us of two contexts in
Deuteronomy specially significant for the plot of Joshua: Joshua's commissioning (Deut 31:1-8) and an extended reflection
on the connection between obedience and blessing, disobedience and curses (Deut 11:1-32). Yahweh's first words, revealing Moses' death and exhorting Joshua to cross "this Jordan,"
allude subtly to Yahweh's telling Moses that not he but Joshua
would lead the people across "this Jordan" (*hayyarden hazzeh*
—found only here in Josh 1:2 and Deut 31:2). Allusions to
Joshua's commissioning in Deuteronomy 31 continue in Yahweh's three-fold admonition to him to be "strong and resolute"
(vss. 6a, 7a, 9b) echoing similar words to Moses (Deut 31:6, 7,

23). In this way both continuity with and disjunction from the Mosaic era are affirmed.

The remainder of Yahweh's speech initiates the plot of obedience. The promise of land and divine aid, given in 1:3-5, is a virtual repetition of Deut 11:24-25.

> Every place on which the soul of your foot treads I have given you, as I said to Moses. From the desert and Lebanon to the great river, the Euphrates—all the land of the Hittites—and as far the Great Sea, this shall be your territory. No one will stand against you all the days of your life. As I was with Moses, I will be with you. I will not forsake you or abandon you. (Josh 1:3-5)

> Every place on which the soul of your foot treads shall be yours. From the desert and Lebanon, from the Euphrates to the western sea, this shall be your territory. No one will stand against you. Yahweh your God will put the dread of you and the fear of you upon all the land on which you tread, as he spoke to you. (Deut 11:24-25)

The Deuteronomic passage is connected with a number of admonitions that emphasize the correlation between obedience to the commandments and successful possession of the promised land (Deut 11:22-23; cf. 11:8, 26-28). The allusion to this text links the two literary contexts, reinforcing the admonition to "be careful to obey all the instruction" of Moses (Josh 1:7).

Yahweh's opening speech reiterates the promise of the land and once again connects its fulfillment to a meticulous obedience to Yahweh's commandments given through Moses. The point is made repeatedly to Joshua:

> Be strong and resolute, because it is you who will cause this people to inherit the land which I swore to their ancestors to give them. However, be strong and very resolute to do carefully all the instruction which Moses my servant commanded you. Do not divert from it to the right or the left, so that you may prevail everywhere you go. Do not let the book of the instruction be absent from your mouth. Meditate on it day and night so that you may carefully do all that is written in it. For then you will be successful in the way you go and will prevail. Have I not commanded you? Be strong and resolute! Do not

be alarmed or terrified, for Yahweh your God is with you wherever you go. (Josh 1:6-9)

Beginning and ending this passage, exhortations call Joshua to obey determinedly Yahweh's commandments; and the intervening material underscores Yahweh's *conditional* participation in the task of possessing the land. Joshua is told that he will bring the people into their inheritance (vs. 6b), but the promise is qualified ("however," *raq*) by an admonition to observe carefully the instructions of Moses (vs. 7a). The connection between obedience and success is then explicitly repeated, not once but twice (for the benefit of Joshua or the reader?). The first admonition is simple and direct; walking the straight and narrow will bring success (vs. 7b). The second drives the point home with repetitive detail: continual meditation on Moses' instruction is necessary in order to implement Yahweh's commandments correctly, and that implementation is necessary for success and fulfillment (vs. 8).

Since Israel is preparing to enter the land, those commandments concerning contact with the inhabitants are particularly relevant. The people of the land, as well as their property, are to be annihilated. Israel may not make a treaty or enter into marriage with them. No gold or silver may be taken as plunder (Deut 7:1-6, 24-26; Exod 34:15). As in other situations, Moses declares that obedience will bring blessing but disobedience will bring calamity (7:4, 9-16).

Through Yahweh's opening speech, then, the narrator introduces obedience as a primary criterion for achieving a desirable ending. Desire for the end (possession of the land) is thus expressed as a desire for obedience, defining the contours of a plot soon to unfold, and setting that plot firmly in place.

Yahweh's exhortations are replayed, in a minor key, in the final speech (vss. 16-18). The four speeches of the chapter form a chiastic structure around Joshua's role as speaker and listener:

Joshua as listener (to Yahweh; vss. 2-9)
    Joshua as speaker (to the officers; vss. 10-11)
    Joshua as speaker (to the eastern tribes; vss. 12-15)
Joshua as listener (to the eastern tribes; vss. 16-18)

The eastern tribes occupy a place corresponding to that of Yahweh, and they respond to Joshua with an ironic rendition of Yahweh's speech. Whereas Yahweh had explained that he would be with Joshua if Joshua was obedient to the instruction of Moses, the eastern tribes reverse the order, declaring that they will be obedient insofar as Yahweh is with Joshua.

> Just as we listened to Moses in everything, so shall we listen to you. However (*raq*) Yahweh must be with you as he was with Moses. (1:17)

Furthermore, Yahweh's speech frames the connection between obedience and fulfillment in positive terms: if Joshua remains obedient he will prosper. However, the eastern tribes put the issue of obedience in negative terms:

> Anyone who rebels against your word and does not obey what you say, in anything you command us, will be put to death. (1:18a)

The eastern tribes even qualify their promised participation with the very words Yahweh used to qualify his participation with Israel: "however, be strong and resolute" (vs. 18b; cf. vs. 7a). Yet their irony cuts most deeply when they allude to rebellion. The idiomatic phrase *yamreh 'et-pika* ("cause your mouth to rebel") has occurred only three times previously. In each instance it refers to Israel's refusal to obey the commandment to enter the land (Deut 1:26, 43; 9:23). The irony arises from the fact that the eastern tribes have previously been accused of discouraging Israel from entering the land (Num 32:7, 14, 15). Now these same tribes who have elected to remain outside the land represent all Israel in declaring allegiance and obedience! Their pious response turns out to be an altered version of Yahweh's initial exhortation. This irony foreshadows the reversal of other expectations and hints at the possibility of other, less desirable conclusions.[1]

RAHAB: A FORBIDDEN OATH

Following the response of the eastern tribes, the text shifts abruptly to a narrative mode in order to recount Israel's first contact with the inhabitants of the land: the account of the spies' encounter with Rahab the harlot (2:1-24). Throughout the history of interpretation, Rahab has been highly regarded. In the New Testament, she is presented as an example of faith and redemption (Heb 11:31; Jas 2:25; Matt 1:5), while in Jewish folklore she becomes the wife of Joshua and the mother of eight prophets![2] Modern scholars have continued to view Rahab in a positive light. Contemporary interpreters have declared Rahab to be "inspired by Yahweh," acclaiming Yahweh's praises and intervening on behalf of Yahweh's people (McCarthy 1971:173). She is a heroine who contributes to Israel's victory, and a "paradigm of hope" for later generations (Hamlin 1983:18). From a different perspective, she represents Israel from the perspective of non-Israel; in her exception she receives a dispensation of mercy from an Israel who has also been the recipient of mercy (Polzin 1980:85-91).

Historical-critical interpretation has focused not so much on Rahab as on the general tone of the story, which, again, is regarded positively. The story of Rahab, we are told, affirms Yahweh's participation in Israel's holy war. It is placed in this context to confirm the will and working of Yahweh, thus providing the divine assurances without which holy war cannot begin.[3] The episode demonstrates Israel's craftiness by showing how a "common prostitute" is "no match for Israel's spies" and has been placed at the beginning of the conquest narratives "to introduce the theology of conquest" (Butler 1983:34-35).

However, when read against the backdrop of the just-articulated Mosaic framework, the episode is also dark and disturbing. The entire incident relates a situation expressly forbidden to Israel and articulates an opposition to the introductory affirmations of obedience.

No sooner have the eastern tribes voiced their pledges of allegiance than the narrator abruptly shifts to a terse narrative report.

> Joshua son of Nun secretly sent two men, spies, from Shittim and said to them, "Go and look over the land, especially Jericho." So they went and came to the house of a woman, a prostitute named Rahab, and they lay down there. (2:1)

The narrator, in the space of a few sentences, creates an ominous mood. The first piece of data concerns the strategy to be employed: Joshua adopts the practice of his predecessor and sends out spies to reconnoiter the land. This strategy, of course, has been tried before, with disastrous results (Deut 1:19-40; Num 14:1-25).

The narrator also provides information about the place of the mission's departure. It is Shittim, a place eliciting repressed memories of apostasy and divine wrath. At Shittim, Israel consorted with the women of Moab, who led the people to turn from Yahweh and worship the Baal of Peor (Num 25:1-5). The wrath of Yahweh had been kindled there, leading to the execution of Israel's leaders. Furthermore, if Shittim may be equated with Abel-Shittim,[4] we will also recognize it as the site where Moses outlined the program for the possession of Canaan (Num 33:48-56). These words of Moses, so recently affirmed in the exhortations to Joshua, echo as the spies depart.

> If you do not dispossess the inhabitants of the land before you, then those you permit to remain will become barbs in your eyes and thorns in your sides, and they will trouble you in the land in which you live. Then what I intended to do to them I will do to you. (Num 33:55-56)

The spies thus leave Shittim, where the people of Israel had "prostituted themselves" with foreign women (Num 25:1), and travel to the house of a prostitute who lives in Canaan. The geographical move to Jericho is a linear one, but in terms of Israel's story the movement represents a return to a troubling place. In a symbolic sense, Rahab is a synthesis of all that is most threatening to Israel, a point which the narrator underscores by the names given her: woman, prostitute, Rahab.

As a woman of Canaan and a prostitute, Rahab signifies the temptation to apostatize. Israel has been warned about the dangers of contact with non-Israelites—especially women (Deut 7:3). Pagan women have the power to lure Israel from obedience to Yahweh to the worship of other deities, a power illustrated at Shittim and affirmed throughout biblical narrative (Judg 3:6; 1 Kgs 11:1-8). Prostitution, likewise, serves as a metaphor for the violation of Yahweh's covenant (Exod 34:14-

16; Deut 31:16-18; Judg 2:17), a peril personified by this person who shelters the spies.[5]

Perhaps more threatening is the fact that the woman has a name. Up to this point the inhabitants of the land have been nameless. Her name is revealing. The name "Rahab" (*rahav*) is identical to the Hebrew adjective meaning "broad" or "wide." This adjective occurs rarely in Genesis through Kings, but in each instance it is employed in connection with the land ("a good and broad land, a land flowing with milk and honey," Exod 3:8; cf. Gen 34:21; Judg 18:10). The land signifies rest and plenitude for Israel. Rahab, however, is an avatar of the land's darker side—the land as seductress, promising fulfillment apart from Yahweh and Yahweh's commandments, sheltering Israel yet luring it into forbidden intrigues. Canaan is, indeed, a land of milk and honey, but it may yet be a land that "devours its inhabitants" (Num 13:32).

The spies, it seems, succumb immediately to Rahab's seductive powers. They "come to" (*wayyabo'u*) her house and "lie down" (*wayyishkevu-shamma*). The verbs have strong sexual overtones. The verb *bo'* is often used to signify a man coming to a woman for the purpose of sexual intercourse (Gen 6:4; 16:2; 30:3; 38:8-9; Deut 22:13; 1 Sam 12:24; 16:21; Ezek 23:44; Prov 6:29), and the king's messengers use it to characterize the spies' activity at Rahab's house, repeating it three times (vs. 3b). The verb *shakav* is more strongly suggestive; to "lie with" (*shakav 'im/'et*) is a common idiom for sexual intercourse (Gen 34:7; 39:7, 10, 12; Exod 22:16; Num 5:13; Deut 22:23; 28:30; 2 Sam 12:11; etc.).[6]

Commentators have generally exhibited an unusual prudishness at this point. After all, this is not the kind of behavior we might have expected to follow the earlier admonitions to obedience! Some have attempted to deflect the narrator's sexual innuendo by suggesting that to call Rahab a *zonah* may simply mean that she was an innkeeper (an interpretation at least as old as the Targum).[7] Others argue that the spies chose to hide out in a brothel because it would be the best place to gather information without attracting notice![8] Such interpretations notwithstanding, we are still left with the impression that Israel enters the land and immediately engages in forbidden activity with the very people who are to be destroyed without mercy. The narrator chooses not to elaborate what the spies do at the house of Rahab, preferring to tantalize the reader with hints of impropriety. The attempts of interpreters to mitigate the suggestion of sexual activity demonstrates that the tactic is indeed effective in creating a disturbing and threatening atmosphere. The tone of the narrative is thus effectively set. Things have begun badly, and not at all according to the plot agenda to which the reader has been introduced.

As the story unfolds, further reversals appear. The king of Jericho, having learned of the spies and their mission, sends a contingent to Rahab's house. The king's men issue a strong demand designed to convince her of the reliability of their intelligence network:

> Bring out the men who came to you—who came to your house—because they have come to reconnoiter the entire land. (2:3)

At this point, the narrator momentarily shifts the reader's point of view to the rooftop, where Rahab has hidden the spies, and then returns immediately to the conversation between Rahab and the king's men (vs. 4a). After the conversation, the narrator interrupts again, taking the reader once more to the hiding Israelites (vs. 6), and then returning to Rahab as the king's men depart (vs. 7).[9] This technique of shifting point of view accomplishes two purposes. First, the narrator is able to build suspense by juxtaposing the images of the suspicious police and the hiding spies. Will Rahab reveal the hiding place? Will the king's men search the house and discover them? Secondly, by focusing the reader's attention on both scenes at once, the narrator is able to accentuate the spies' precarious dependence on Rahab. Their survival is dependent on her disposition toward them.

Rahab does not challenge the messengers (a response that would certainly invite a search) and admits that the spies have indeed visited her house. Her ready agreement is a ploy to establish her credibility before the king's men, so that the rest of her report may ring true. Her words are brief and forceful, giving the messengers little opportunity to question or reflect.

> And she said, "Yes, the men came to me, but I did not know from whence they came. When the gate closed for the night the men left. I don't know where the men went. Quick, get after them. You can certainly catch them!" (2:4b-5)

Responding with her own imperative, Rahab deftly dispatches the messengers on a course that will prove no threat to the spies. Without even entering the house, the king's men obey Rahab and depart in hot pursuit of the Israelites.

The king's men are clearly no match for Rahab. Neither, it is increasingly apparent, are the Israelite spies. Notice the passive role the spies play in the scene: "the woman had taken the two men and had hidden them" (vs. 4a). Rahab is dominant and assertive. She is now "the woman" giving shelter to "the men."[10] In contrast, the spies of Israel remain passive both here and throughout the entire episode.[11] They are sent by Joshua (and will later be sent by Rahab, vs. 21b). Their first activity is to "lie down." They have nothing to say about how the threat from the king's men will be met. The narrator tells us only that they are "taken" and "hidden."

The episode intimates reversals of another sort as well, as it alludes to an earlier story about messengers who were hidden from the threatening people of the city, namely, the story of Sodom's destruction (Gen. 19:1-29).[12] Both narratives tell of a city doomed to destruction. Two men arrive in the city and are given shelter by one of its citizens. Later in the evening, while they are at the house, the men of the city appear at the door. They demand that the strangers be brought out, but are quickly dispatched. The city is subsequently destroyed, but the citizen in whose house the men had stayed is spared, along with their entire family.

The narrator plays with elements of the story of Sodom, suggesting correspondences in some cases but eliciting contrasts in others. One cannot but appreciate the subtlety with which this is done. The two men who arrive in Sodom (mal'akim; "messengers/angels" in Gen 19:1,15 and in Josh 6:17, 25) intend to spend the night in the city plaza (*rahov*). The two men who come to Jericho stay in the house of Rahab (*rahav*). When the men of the city demand that Lot bring the men out (*hotsi-'em*), Lot responds by offering to give them his daughters, who have not "known" (*yad'u*) a man (Gen 19:8). Rahab responds to the same demand by declaring pointedly that she does not know (*yada'ti*) who the men are or where they have gone (Josh 2:4, 5).[13]

Rahab's situation is, however, quite different than Lot's. The men who come to Sodom are sent to rescue Lot from the coming destruction. Lot is hesitant to leave and pleads with the messengers to allow him to stay in the region (Gen 19:18-20), prompting the messengers to exempt the village of Zoar (vss. 21-22). Lot is also unsuccessful in collecting some of his family (vs. 14), and, during the conflagration, loses his wife (vs. 26). On the other hand, the two men who arrive in Jericho are sent to reconnoiter in preparation for its destruction. Rahab pleads with the men, but in contrast to Lot, her pleas express an urgent determination to be spared (Josh 2:12). As a result, the spies exempt Rahab and her entire family, all of whom eventually escape the destruction of the city (6:23). As a whole, Rahab acquits herself much more favorably than does Lot, whose rescue is undertaken because of his relation to Abraham (Gen 19:29). The story of Rahab is thus rendered in a way that not only reverses stereotypical gender roles (Rahab speaks for her household) but challenges notions of grace and election (cf. Deut 9:4-6). The correspondences elicit a mood of sinfulness, wrath, and doom.

As soon as Rahab sends the king's men away, she returns to the rooftop, where she has hidden the spies under stalks of flax. The narrator continues to contrast the passivity of the spies with Rahab's determination to dictate events. The spies continue to be a whirlwind of activity—they are once again preparing to "lie down" (vs. 8a). It seems they have no particular plan in mind. Rahab, however, has a definite agenda. The narrator signals her resolve in two clipped phrases: "she went up to the roof and said to the men" (vs. 8b). Her initial words are meant to disarm the spies, who must now be aware that they have been discovered.

> I know that Yahweh has given you the land and that your terror has fallen on us; all the inhabitants of the land have despaired because of you. We have heard how Yahweh dried up the waters of the Red Sea before you when you came out of Egypt and what you did to the two kings of the Amorite on the other side of the Jordan—Sihon and Og, whom you put under the ban. We heard and our hearts melted, and everyone lost their nerve because of you, for Yahweh your god is God in the sky above and the earth below. (2:9b-11)

One must wonder if Rahab's "I know" here is uttered with the same heart-felt candor as the "I do not know" she has spoken to the king's men. Her words and actions belie the image of a panic-stricken opponent, resigned to the coming cataclysm. Rahab may be aware that the city is doomed, but she clearly recognizes an opportunity to save herself and her family. Her speech is methodical, her plan of action is coolly executed, and her words are calculated to gain the confidence of the two spies in what, for them, must be a difficult predicament.

Even more remarkable is Rahab's acquaintance with Israel's hymnody. She knows what Yahweh has done for Israel, and she knows the songs Israel sings to Yahweh. As she reviews Yahweh's mighty deeds, Rahab quotes a relevant passage from the "Song of Moses" (Exod 15:1-18).

> Your terror has fallen on us
> And all the inhabitants of the land have despaired
> > because of you. (Josh 2:9)

> All the inhabitants of Canaan will despair.
> Upon them will fall your terror and dread.
> > (Exod 15:15b-16a)

Rahab knows Moses' commandments as well.

> For Yahweh your god is God in the sky above and the earth below. (Josh 2:11b)
> Acknowledge today and take to your heart that Yahweh is God in the sky above and the earth below. There is no other. (Deut 4:39)

One might have expected such words from faithful Israel as it prepares itself for the campaigns ahead. Through the mouth of one of the accursed inhabitants of the land, however, the words are discordant and confusing.[14] Perhaps that is the effect the narrator intends. Is Rahab so different than those who have come to slay her? Who is more worthy of salvation, these Israelites whose memory is short, or this Canaanite, who acclaims the works of Yahweh and aggressively seeks a gracious response?

Having finished her introductory remarks, Rahab gets to the point. The shift in intention is signaled by an introductory 'attah, expressing the urgency of her demands. Her speech is again governed by an imperative.

> And now, swear to me by Yahweh, because I have been loyal to you, that you will be loyal to the house of my father, that you will give me a sign of truth, that you will spare my father, my mother, my brother, my sister, and all those with them, and that you will deliver us from death. (2:12-13)

Rahab's request is bold, and she makes it forcefully. She first reminds the spies what she has done for them. Her reminder also highlights the delicate nature of the current situation; Rahab's "loyalty" may quickly vanish if her request is not granted. So that the point will not be missed, she emphatically defines the spies' role in the relationship: "you, even you, must be loyal to the house of my father." Then Rahab presses her advantage, pushing them to accept a four-fold oath. The oath is detailed and is designed to cover all possible loopholes and contingencies. It is not merely redundant. Rahab wants to be certain that Israel will be able to find no opening by which to abrogate the oath.

Although the spies seem lethargic, they are quick to catch the implications of Rahab's demand and immediately agree to the terms of the oath.

> The men said to her, "Our lives in place of yours to the death! If you do not divulge this situation, then, when Yahweh gives us the land, we will be loyal and faithful to you." (2:14)

Rahab has given appropriate glory to Yahweh, but it appears that the spies are concerned only about saving their lives. So concerned are they, in fact, that they are willing, without hesitation, to abandon obedience to Yahweh's commandments for the sake of an expedient resolution to their predicament. There are no acclamations here about Yahweh's ability to save! Rahab has displayed the faith, resourcefulness, and sense of purpose that ought to characterize Israel in its acquisition of Canaan. The spies, it appears, are wanting.

The story of the spies and Rahab is an antithesis of the construct of obedience and faith presented by the introductory speeches in Joshua 1. Having entered the land in preparation for subjugating it, the two Israelite spies have themselves been mastered and ensnared by their Canaanite counterpart. Now the unthinkable has happened. An agreement, confirmed by oath, has been made with an inhabitant of the land. And there are strong indications in the structure and content of Rahab's speech that the agreement is in fact a covenant.[15] This new relationship represents a serious infraction of Moses' commandments, and the reader must wonder how such a situation will be resolved. Will Israel find a way to break the spies' oath and thus fulfill Yahweh's commandment? Will the oath be honored, exempting Rahab and her family from the ban but threatening the promise of the land?

Once the oath has been made, Rahab facilitates the spies' escape by lowering them out the window of her house. She then gives them important instructions for their escape. Once again she speaks to them with imperatives.

> She lowered them through the window with a rope, because her house was in the city wall and she lived in the wall. She said to them, "Go to the hill country so those who are pursuing you won't overtake you. Hide there for three days until those who are looking for you return. After that, you can go on your way." (2:15-16)

We gain the impression that Rahab's instructions are given to the men as they are lowered down the wall. The image rendered is unusual and has elicited a number of explanations from commentators who think the scene too awkward.[16] And yet, what could be more appropriate than the spectacle of the two spies dangling, like Jonathan Edwards' spider, at the end of a rope held by their redemptress?

Once the spies are clear of imminent danger they seem to have second thoughts about the oath they have just made.

> The men said to her, "We are innocent of this, your oath, which you made us swear! Look, we are coming into the land. Tie this scarlet thread in the window from which you lowered us. Gather your father, mother, brother, and all the house of your father to yourself in the house. Anyone who goes out from the doors of your house, their blood will be on their head. We will not be obligated. Also, if you divulge this business of ours we will not be obligated to your oath which you made us swear." (2:17-20)

Rahab was right to observe such detail in fixing the terms of the oath. The Israelites are already looking for a way out. Their remarks plainly deny responsibility for the oath. It is, they assert at beginning and end, "your oath which you made us swear" (vss. 17, 20). Three times they repeat "We are innocent" (naqi; vss. 17, 19, 20), as if the oath could be nullified by the claim that it was made under duress.

The irony of the spies' disavowal is enhanced by the many possible connotations of the Hebrew term naqi. Used of an oath, naqi signifies a release of obligation (Gen 24:21), but it can also denote a state of ethical blamelessness (Exod 23:7; Job 4:7; Ps 15:5). The term most frequently occurs in combination with dam to signify wrongful death ("innocent blood"). The response of the spies allows all these nuances to be brought into play. The spies are clearly trying to shake off their responsibility for making the oath, and they set conditions which might void it.[17] Yet, on another level, they are maintaining their righteousness in regard to Yahweh's statutes. "This was not our fault," they seem to say. "This is Rahab's oath, and she made us swear to it." Finally, the repetition of naqi puts a twist on the spies' assertion that anyone who leaves the house will be responsible for his or her own blood (vs. 19). Is innocent blood to be shed here? Whose blood is innocent?

The spies also stipulate that Rahab must tie a strand of scarlet cord (*tiqwat hut hashshani hazzeh*) in her window, presumably as a signal to the invading Israelites that her house is exempt from the ban (vs. 18). This small detail has intrigued many readers. What does the scarlet thread symbolize? Does it recall the blood of the Passover lamb on the doorposts of Israel's houses?[18] Or is the scarlet cord a contemporary signpost for a city's red-light district?[19] There is a simpler answer. The scarlet cord (*tiqwat hashshani*, vs. 21) is actually a pun in code. The cord (*tiqwat*) is a sign of Rahab's waiting or hope (*tiqwat*). And it is scarlet (*shani*) because it is a signal to the two (*shney*) men who have made the oath.[20]

By their protests to Rahab the spies both tacitly admit that she has prevailed and try to mitigate the seriousness of the transgression which their oath represents. By her aggressive opportunism, Rahab has manipulated the Israelites into an act which seriously breaches the covenant with Yahweh and which therefore threatens a fulfilling ending. The spies can do little more than make feeble modifications to the oath, and Rahab quickly agrees. Then she dismisses them (vs. 21) and ties the cord in her window (vs. 22).

At this point, one may well wonder how the threats embodied by Rahab and her oath are going to be met. How can such a disruption be worked through, so that an undesirable or premature end can be avoided? The text affords no immediate resolution. The narrator quickly transports the reader back across the Jordan, where Joshua and the rest of Israel await the return of the spies. The spies give a brief report.

> Yahweh has indeed given the entire land into our hand. Moreover, all the inhabitants of the land are in despair because of us. (2:24)

These are bold and confident assertions, and we may assume that they are accepted as such by those who listen. The spies are much more courageous when they are safe! But the reader has seen both the spies and the land from another angle. There is danger in the land, a fact which the spies do not articulate. They have been so completely overwhelmed by Rahab's wiles that they can do nothing but parrot her words in a highly ironic fashion. Like the king's men, the spies' perception is dictated by Rahab's speech. Their report is not their own, but Rahab's, and as we have seen, Rahab has quite a way with words.

FROM JORDAN TO JERICHO

The portrait of disobedient Israel is now countered by a series of episodes bringing together the narrative's most powerful signifiers of obedience: Israel crosses the Jordan in strict obedience to the words of Moses and then confirms its fidelity by observing both a ceremony of circumcision and the festival of Passover (3:1-5:12). The crossing narrative itself devotes considerable attention to the liturgical aspects of Israel's entry into the land.[21] By rendering this story in the form of a liturgical narrative, the crossing is presented as a sacral act, effectively affirming Israel's loyalty to Yahweh.

Much of the episode is structured according to a detailed command/execution framework which reinforces and advances the plot of obedient Israel as it enters the land to obtain Yahweh's promise. At various points throughout the crossing, Joshua gives commands or instructions (or Yahweh gives commands through Joshua), and the narrator duly notes the execution of these commands. A few examples are illustrative.[22]

> Joshua said to the priests, "Lift up the Ark of the Covenant and cross over before the people." So they lifted up the Ark of the Covenant and went before the people. (3:6)

> Joshua said to them, "Cross over before the Ark of Yahweh your God into the middle of the Jordan. Each man is to take up one stone on his shoulder, according to the number of tribes of the Israelites . . . ."
> And the Israelites did so, just as Joshua commanded. They carried twelve stones from the middle of the Jordan, as Yahweh directed Joshua, according to the number of tribes of Israelites. (4:5, 8b)

> Yahweh said to Joshua, "Command the priests who are carrying the Ark of the Testimony to come out of the Jordan." So Joshua commanded the priests, "Come out of the Jordan."

> And when the priests who were carrying the Ark came out of
> the Jordan . . . . (4:15-18a)

The obedience of Israel is also suggested by the central place given in the narrative to the Ark of the Covenant. The Ark symbolizes the leadership of Yahweh, and as Israel follows the Ark into the Jordan its obedience is likewise symbolized and affirmed. The Ark remains in the Jordan until "the fulfillment of every word which Yahweh commanded Joshua to tell the people, according to everything which Moses commanded Joshua" (4:10b-c).[23] The sign which accompanies the entrance and departure of the Ark—the drying up of the Jordan and the return of the waters—confirms again the connection between Israel's obedience and the successful appropriation of the promise of the land; a connection which Joshua explicitly confirms in 3:10-13.

Israel's proper and timely performance of religious rituals provides a final confirmation of its obedience. Rites of circumcision are performed upon Israel's entrance into Canaan, and the Passover feast is observed. Both observances implicitly seal Yahweh's promise and election of Israel, as well as Israel's acceptance of the promise and obligations of election.

Even within these episodes, however, which stridently affirm Israel's obedience and fidelity to Yahweh, there are intimations that contrary currents run beneath the surface. The root 'br, meaning to cross over or through, occurs 22 times in Joshua 3 and 4. Its frequent use is not surprising, of course, given the context. But the term can also signify a darker crossing—the "transgression" of the covenant with Yahweh (Josh 7:11, 13; 23:16; Judg 2:20; 2 Kgs 18:12). Its repetition, therefore, is a subliminal reminder that the threatening tensions released in the previous episode concerning Rahab have yet to be resolved.

This sense of dissonance is increased when the narrator offers a brief aside after Israel has finished crossing over the Jordan.

> When all the kings of the Amorites, on the west side of the
> Jordan, and all the kings of the Canaanites, near the sea,
> heard that Yahweh had dried up the water of the Jordan

before the Israelites until they could cross it, their hearts melted and they lost their nerve because of the Israelites. (5:1)

The words, of course, are parallel to Rahab's (2:9-11). The dissonance continues as the circumcision ceremony at Gibeath Haaraloth is related (5:4-8). The narrative has been continuing in its command/execution mode (vss. 2-3). At this point, however, the narrator abruptly digresses in order to reiterate the sad story of the failure of the wilderness generation.

> For forty years the Israelites wandered in the desert, until the entire nation came to an end—the warriors who had come out of Egypt, who did not obey Yahweh. Yahweh swore to them that they would not see the land which Yahweh swore to their ancestors to give us, a land flowing with milk and honey. (5:6)

The wilderness generation presents a powerful metaphor of disobedience and failure; they did not obey Yahweh and were brought to a landless end.

The siege of Jericho (6:1-27) brings the two opposing plot lines into direct conflict. Will the ban be executed? Will Rahab and her family be spared? Once again, the campaign is enacted through ritual, complete with Ark, priests, and following Israelites. Yahweh commands Israel to march around Jericho for seven days, led by seven priests carrying trumpets. On the seventh day, Israel is to march around the city seven times, with the priests blowing the trumpets (6:3-4, 15-16). The procedure undoubtedly has ritual significance, but the multiplication of sevens is particularly appropriate given the circumstances of the spies' previous visit. The seven (*sheba'*) priests, days, and circuits around Jericho are symbolic repetitions of the forbidden oath (*shebua'*) which has been made between Rahab and Israel. The instructions thus display a certain irony and, since they are given by Yahweh, indicate that the spies' tryst with Rahab has not gone unnoticed.

Before Israel prepares to take the city, Joshua makes a ruling on the oath (6:17). Rahab and her family are to be spared. He makes, however, no mention of the oath. In the people's presence, he gives the impression that exempting her is an act of gratitude and mercy rather than one of obligation.

However, Rahab the prostitute is to be spared, both she and
everyone with her in the house, because she hid the emissaries we sent. (16:17b)

When speaking privately to the spies, however, Joshua
acknowledges the real reason for her exemption (that is, Israel
is bound by oath; vs. 22). Fidelity to the oath will take prece-
dence over the strict application of the ban. Joshua sanctions
what the spies have done, effectively countermanding Moses'
commandments which, at the beginning, he was admonished to
observe.

The siege is a success, nevertheless, and the ostensive plot
line is maintained. Israel acts in perfect obedience to the instructions of Yahweh given through Joshua, and the entire encounter with Jericho is not so much a battle as "a ritual cultic act"
(McKenzie 1966:53). Yahweh delivers the people of Jericho into
Israel's hands and the ban is applied to the city.

Rahab and her family are exempted by Joshua's command.
Joshua attempts to mitigate this awkward situation by assigning
Rahab's family to a place "outside the camp" (6:23). The verb
employed here (nuah) is also used to signify the fulfillment Israel
seeks in the land (Deut 12:10; Josh 1:15; 21:42; 22:4; 23:1).
Ironically, Rahab now has what Israel seeks. By putting Rahab
outside the camp, the threat she embodies is addressed but
glossed. Rahab's part in the story ends on an ominous note:
"she lives in the midst of Israel to this very day" (vs. 25). Israel
has been seduced by Canaan. Is Joshua's ruling a sufficient
remedy?

ACHAN: THE BAN TRANSGRESSED

The city of Ai is the target of the next campaign, but before the
episode begins, the narrator offers a disturbing bit of information.

The Israelites committed a violation against the ban. Achan
son of Carmi son of Zabdi son of Zerah, of the tribe of Judah,
took some of what had been placed under the ban. Then the
anger of Yahweh burned against the Israelites. (7:1)

Disaster is no longer potential. Israel's disobedience, and the frightful consequences of that disobedience, are now explicitly articulated. As with Jericho, spies are sent out on a reconnaissance mission to Ai. They return with the bold assessment that only a fraction of the Israelite force will be needed to overwhelm the city. Their report exudes confidence.

> They returned to Joshua and said to him, "All the people need not go up. Let about two or three thousand go up and attack Ai. Let not all the people exert themselves there, because they are few. (7:3)

Israel's confidence, however, turns out to be ephemeral. Without even the hint of a valiant attack, the reader encounters the following report:

> About three thousand of the people went up there and fled before the men of Ai. (7:4)

The Israelites are routed by the small force at Ai and are chased throughout the countryside (7:5). In a way, this turn of events is not surprising. The people have not consulted Yahweh, nor have they awaited any instructions from their God. In fact, Yahweh is absent from the entire debacle. The roles have been reversed. It is now said of Israel, as it was said previously of the Canaanites, that "the hearts of the people melted like water" (7:6b; cf. 2:24; 5:1). We have yet to encounter any terrified Canaanites.

As with the incident involving Rahab, the disobedience of Israel gives rise to a plot rendered in an ironic mode. Many elements of the episode represent reversals of previous episodes or motifs, and the telling of the story is rich with sarcasm. Furthermore, as in Joshua 2, the dark mood of the text is enhanced by its evocation of destructive imagery. In both structure and vocabulary, the episode recalls the two events that Deuteronomy lifts up as the salient examples of Israel's disobedience: Israel's grumbling at Kadesh (and their defeat at Hormah; Deut 1:26-46) and the worship of the golden calf (Deut 9:7-10:11).[24] The strong correspondences with these Deuteronomic texts puts the story of Achan against the backdrop of rebellion and idolatry, and hints at exclusion from the land and the visitation of Yahweh's anger. Rendered thus, the story of Achan counters the depiction of an obedient Israel.

Even Joshua, whose image has remained relatively untarnished to this point, becomes an ironic figure—a virtual antitype of Moses. At Israel's defeat, Joshua immediately rends his garments and falls down before the Ark, where he remains until the evening (vs. 6). He then intercedes with Yahweh on behalf of Israel.

> Joshua said, "Alas, my lord Yahweh! Why did you ever bring this people across the Jordan—to give us into the hands of the Amorites to destroy us? If only we had decided to live on the other side of the Jordan! By your leave, my Lord, what can I say now that Israel has turned its back in the presence of its enemies? Now the Canaanites, and all who live in the land, will envelop us and cut off our name from the land. What will you do for the sake of your great name?" (7:7-9)

Both the speech and the scenario are reminiscent of a previous event: the return of the twelve spies to Moses after they had reconnoitered the land (Num 14:1ff). In that instance as well, Joshua had *rent* his garments (14:6) while Moses had fallen face down to intercede for Israel. Joshua's response to the situation casts him in the intercessory role of Moses. He even seems to have learned a few tricks from Moses. Moses had been able to dissuade Yahweh from bringing an end to Israel by arguing that Yahweh's reputation would be damaged in the eyes of the Egyptians. The Egyptians, Moses had argued, would hear of Israel's destruction and believe that Yahweh was not able to fulfill his promise to bring Israel into the land (Num 14:13-16). Joshua employs a similar strategy. He declares that the Canaanites will hear of Israel's defeat and thus appeals to Yahweh for the sake of Yahweh's "great name."

But it doesn't work this time. Joshua's speech has more in common with the grumbling of the Israelites than with the intercessory prayer of Moses.

> All the Israelites grumbled against Moses and Aaron and the entire congregation said to them, "If only we had died in

> Egypt! If only we had died in this desert! Why does Yahweh
> bring us into this land to fell us by the sword? Our wives and
> children will become plunder. Would it not be better for us to
> return to Egypt?'' (Num 14:2-3)

Having adopted the intercessory role of Moses, Joshua paradoxically echoes the grumbling of Israel, which, in the original
instance, had resulted in the nullification of Yahweh's promise
to bring them into the land (Num 14:11-12, 20-25). Survival is
the issue from Joshua's perspective, not necessarily the maintenance of Yahweh's reputation.

While Moses' persuasive tactics had been effective, Yahweh
is unimpressed by Joshua. In fact, Yahweh's first words are a
rebuff. There is no reason for Joshua to be groveling. Israel has
committed a grave offense. Yahweh's outrage is expressed in
terse language, punctuated by a sequence of verbs detailing the
nature of the offense.

> Yahweh said to Joshua, "Get up! What are you doing, falling
> on your face? Israel has sinned. Moreover, they have trans-
> gressed the covenant which I commanded them; they have
> taken what is under the ban, they have stolen, they have
> hidden, they have put it with their own possessions." (7:10-
> 11)

Yahweh's words shatter the facade of Israelite fidelity and
threaten to bring the story to an abrupt end. Yahweh has
repeatedly warned of dire consequences if such things are done
in Israel. Will Israel, indeed, be destroyed?

Yahweh, however, provides a way for the threat to be
dissipated and issues a new set of commandments. The people
of Israel are to consecrate themselves in preparation for a
sacred assembly (vs. 13a), a command which echoes the one
given to Israel as it prepared to cross ('br) the Jordan into
Canaan (3:5). The Israelites must consecrate themselves again;
this time because one of them has transgressed ('br) the covenant of Yahweh.

Yahweh stipulates a set of procedures for identifying and
punishing the offender (vss. 14-15). The tribes are to present
themselves the next morning, and, in a meticulous process, the
guilty party will be identified by clan and family.[25] Ritual, as a

marker of Israel's faithfulness, once again appears and dissipates the disruptive images of disobedience, so that the plot of obedience can be reasserted.

The magnitude of the threat can be appreciated by virtue of the extreme measures taken to resolve it. The punishment to be meted out is severe.

> The one discovered with the banned items will be burned with fire, along with everything that one has, because that person has transgressed my commandment and has committed a sacrilege in Israel. (7:15)

The means of execution makes a point. Yahweh's instructions correspond to the punishment to be inflicted on a town guilty of leading Israel to worship other deities (Deut 13:13-19), thus linking Achan's transgression with Israel's primal sin.

> You must search out, investigate, and inquire thoroughly. If it is established as true, that this abomination has been done in your midst, then you must severely strike the inhabitants of that city with the edge of the sword. Put it and everything in it under the ban, and put its livestock to the edge of the sword. You are to gather all its plunder in the town square and burn all its plunder with fire as an offering to Yahweh your God. It is to be a mound of rubble forever, not to be rebuilt. (Deut 13:15-17)

This is effectively what happens to Achan once he is identified as the offender. When the stolen goods are brought from his tent, they are spread out before Yahweh. Then Achan, along with "the silver, the robe, the gold crescent, his sons, his daughters, his cattle, his donkey, his sheep, his tent, and everything he had" (vs. 24), are taken to a place outside the camp, where they are destroyed. After all is burned, the Israelites pile a heap of rocks over Achan, which, the reader is told, "is still there today" (vs. 26). This punishment, applied to this offense, signifies the deeper threat which Achan's sin has brought about. Contact with the land has the potential to lead Israel astray from Yahweh to worship other deities.

Before Achan and his family are executed, Joshua pronounces sentence over them.

Joshua said, "As you have troubled us, Yahweh will trouble you today."(7:25a)

Joshua's words are true in one sense, but in another they are ironic. It is Yahweh who has brought "trouble" on Israel, and it is Israel that brings trouble on Achan!

Achan's story is the antithesis of Rahab's. Rahab is an inhabitant of the land and therefore subject to extermination. However, she and her entire family, along with all that they have, are spared (6:23). Achan, on the other hand, is an Israelite, and therefore can expect to receive a possession in the land. However, he and his entire family, along with all that he has, are placed under the ban and destroyed. Rahab hides the Israelite spies on the top of her house. When men are sent to apprehend them, she lies to them so that they do not discover what she has hidden. For this, she is exempted from death. Achan hides the booty of Jericho under his tent, and when men are sent to fetch it, he readily discloses its whereabouts. When the evidence is uncovered, he is killed. Rahab and her family are taken outside the camp and given a place to live. Achan and his family are taken outside the camp and executed.

Both episodes run counter to our expectations. The contrast between Rahab and Achan muddles concepts of election, obedience, and blessing. Are the inhabitants of the land so different than Israel? Who may be eligible for grace? Who for retribution? A sense of this blurring can perhaps be detected in Achan's response to Joshua. When discovered, Achan is enjoined to confess and give praise to Yahweh (vs. 19). Achan readily admits that he has sinned and has coveted the booty of Jericho, and he gives a detailed description of what he has taken and where he has hidden it. Why does he so quickly cooperate? Perhaps he believes that his confession will allow him to receive mercy. After all, had not Joshua been merciful to Rahab, the Canaanite? For his truthful cooperation, however, Achan receives the most severe penalty.

Only after Achan and his family are exterminated does Yahweh's burning anger subside (7:26b; cf. Deut 13:19). The execution of Achan and his family purges the disobedience from

Israel, so that it may continue on its quest for the land. Ritual purification signifies that Israel has returned to obedience and is ready once more to follow Yahweh's instructions. The command/execution framework is again employed in the account of the taking of Ai (8:1-28), and Israel meets with great success. Yahweh reveals the battle plan for another assault on Ai, and it is appropriate in light of Israel's prior conduct. Israel was taken in by deceit at Jericho. Now Yahweh stipulates deceit as the means by which Israel will overcome its foes at Ai.

Israel follows Yahweh's instructions to the letter, achieving a sweeping victory. Ai becomes a mound of rubble forever (Josh 7:28; cf. Deut 13:17) and a pile of rocks is heaped over its king as with Achan (8:29; 7:26).

With Achan and Ai safely interred, the negative tone of the text abruptly shifts to the positive.

> Then Joshua built an altar to Yahweh the God of Israel on Mount Ebal, as Moses the servant of Yahweh had commanded the Israelites. (8:30-31a)

From the heaping of a rock pile, the narrative moves immediately to the building of an altar. The altar symbolizes the presence of Yahweh, and the sacrifices offered on it reaffirm the communion shared between Yahweh and Israel. Moses' words are inscribed on stones, and a ceremony follows in the area of Mounts Ebal and Gerizim, during which his words are read to the assembled tribes of Israel (8:30-35).

Commentators have generally been troubled by the absence of a proper transition and by the sudden shift in tone, geography, and perspective. Some have gone so far as to transplant the passage into another part of the text where it creates a less disturbing effect![26] It seems that the very abruptness with which the text moves to the report sets the passage apart and encourages the reader to give it additional attention. This may be precisely the effect intended, for the report of the ceremony at Ebal serves an important function at a pivotal point in the book; it renders a new beginning and emphatically reestablishes the plot of obedience.

Like Josh 1:1-18, the report of the ceremony at Ebal is a composite of materials drawn from Deuteronomy, this time primarily from chapters 27-31.[27] As with the book's introduction, the words of Moses, and their fulfillment by Joshua, are the focus of attention. In fact, as the narrator repeatedly asserts, the entire episode is undertaken in response to Moses' words: the altar is built, the *torah* is transcribed onto stones, Israel assembles on Ebal and Gerizim, and the words of the *torah* are read, all "as Moses had commanded" (vss. 31, 32, 33, 34). The point is made again at the conclusion of the report, which asserts that "there was not one word, of any that Moses commanded, that Joshua did not read as he faced the entire congregation of Israel" (8:35a).

Thus, at this key juncture in the text, the two motifs which signify the plot of obedient Israel—the words of Moses and ritual observance—are combined, representing a powerful attempt to master the disruptions released in previous incidents and to reorient the story toward the desired end. The narrative explicitly affirms that the people are under blessing, as they had been previously (vs. 33). This reaffirmation of their fidelity means that Israel is again ready to take possession of Canaan. True, the promises are still conditional; the curse is yet a possibility for Israel (vs. 34b). Even so, Israel's obedience has been vigorously reasserted, and the reader has every reason to assume that this new beginning will put to rest any threatening endings.

GIBEON: THE TRANSGRESSION OF THE COVENANT

Up to this point, Israel has encountered very little in the way of coordinated resistance in its campaign against the inhabitants of the land. That is about to change. The narrator opens the next episode with the report that all the kings of the land mobilized their forces, with one accord, to wage war against Joshua and Israel (9:1-2). These are presumably the same quivering kings who had no courage to face Israel when they heard that Yahweh had dried up the Jordan (5:1). Now they hear (we are not told what) and ally themselves against the invaders. There are no reports of panic or despair this time.

There is, however, one city that does not join the coalition:

> The inhabitants of Gibeon heard what Joshua had done to Jericho and Ai. (9:3)

The two previous campaigns began with the sending out of spies to reconnoiter the city (2:1; 7:2). This time, the reader is the spy. The narrator begins by taking the reader into the city which will be the focus of action for the next episode. The change in perspective is clearly marked in the Hebrew text by the use of an intensive pronoun, *gam-hemmah*. This shift is intended to give the reader vital information which will not be available to Joshua and Israel; namely, that the Gibeonites have decided to deceive Israel.

> They acted with cunning and proceeded to take provisions. They took worn-out sacks on their donkeys, along with old wineskins that were cracked and mended, and worn-out, patched sandals on their feet, and wore tattered clothing. All their food was dry and crumbling. They went to Joshua at Gilgal and said to him and the men of Israel, "We have come from a distant land. Make a covenant with us." (9:4-6)

The narrator describes the Gibeonites' appearance at some length but does not reveal the purpose of the ruse until the men have reached Joshua and Israel at Gilgal. The reader therefore knows what Joshua and Israel do not; these men are not what they seem. The information effectively creates suspense. Will Israel recognize the trick this time?

The Gibeonites negotiate with Joshua and "the men of Israel."[28] The conversation has something of the cat-and-mouse patter that characterized the spies' encounter with Rahab. There is no hint of a salutation. Rather, the Gibeonites' introduction is terse and pointed. Giving only minimal information, they immediately press for a treaty. The first sentence, "we have come from a distant land," seems a slight justification for the strongly worded imperative, "now, make a treaty with us." The phrase used here, *karat l-*, has occurred in only three previous contexts, all of which expressly warn Israel against making treaties with the inhabitants of Canaan (Exod 23:32;

34:12, 15; Deut 7:2; cf. Judg 2:2). There is danger here, and Israel's record does not engender confidence.

The reader, by now, is aware that Israel is susceptible to imperatives. In this case, however, there is no predicament to force a decision, and the response is more cautious.

> The men of Israel said to the Hivites, "Perhaps you live in our midst. How could we make a treaty with you?" (9:7)

The use of the term "Hivites" to denote the Gibeonite emissaries underscores the perilous nature of the conversation and reminds the reader that Israel may not perceive what is apparent. The content of the response, however, indicates that the Israelite leaders are somewhat skeptical of the Gibeonites' claim and intentions. If these emissaries actually live nearby, any kind of a treaty would be out of the question.

The leaders' question is a dangerous one, and the Gibeonites know it; if given the opportunity for conjecture the ruse may be uncovered. They therefore evade both question and questioners. Instead, they turn from the leaders to address Joshua, presenting themselves as "your servants" (vs. 8a). The reversal of common syntax ("your servants are we"; 'avdekem 'anahnu) focuses attention on the relationship which the emissaries propose, while the use of the second person pronoun is clearly intended to appeal directly to Joshua. The emissaries are, in effect, offering themselves (and thus their city) to Joshua as vassals.[29] The appeal is simple and direct, shifting attention away from their place of origin, while at the same time elaborating the benefits of the proposed treaty.

The tactic is not entirely successful. Joshua continues to question them, although with less specificity than did the leaders of Israel.

> But Joshua said to them, "Who are you, and where do you come from?" (9:8b)

Again the Gibeonites give a vague reply which emphasizes their claim to come from a distance ("from a very distant land," vs. 9a), and again deflect the inquiry. Israel must be given no time to consider the possibility that the emissaries do indeed "live in their midst." The Gibeonites therefore bring up a subject sure to enhance their status.

> They said to him, "Your servants have come from a very distant land because of the name of Yahweh your God, for we have received the news of all he did in Egypt, and all he did to the two kings of the Amorites on the other side of the Jordan; Sihon king of Heshbon and Og the king of Bashan who was in Ashtaroth." (9:9-10)

As with Rahab, the recognition and declaration of Yahweh's deeds issues from the mouths of those whose doom Yahweh has decreed. Also, like Rahab, the Gibeonites are evidently familiar with the Mosaic *torah*. They know that Moses permitted Israel to make peace with cities that are "very distant" (Deut 20:15) and they are now using this knowledge to their advantage.

Next, the emissaries pointedly draw the Israelites' attention to the "evidence" which substantiates their claims, still depicting themselves in the most innocuous manner possible. They have been sent by the elders of their land (the inhabitants of Canaan have kings) to Israel on a mission of peace (vs. 11). Their food and clothing, they maintain, was in good condition when they set out. Now it is badly deteriorated. Their country must, indeed, be very far distant (vss. 12-13).

The text has, to this point, devoted a great deal of space to the actual negotiations, thus heightening the suspense and tension. Yet, as with Rahab, the flow of conversation has been dictated by the inhabitants of the land rather than by Israel. The end of the matter seems a foregone (if unsettling) conclusion.

> The men sampled their provisions but did not consult Yahweh. Joshua made peace with them and made a covenant with them to let them live, and the leaders of the congregation gave them their oath. (9:14-15)

Once again Israel and Joshua appear to have been hoodwinked. But is this really the case?

Although the intentions of the Gibeonites are evident to the reader, the narrative reveals little about the thoughts or perspective of Joshua and the Israelite leaders. Why has Joshua been so quick to make this covenant, and why has it been rubber-stamped by the Israelite leaders? Could Joshua have been so naive as to be unable to see through the Gibeonites crude disguise? One senses a hint of eagerness in Israel's readiness to make a covenant with the Gibeonites. The Israelites sample their provisions, as if to prove the truth of the emissaries' claim. But the narrator describes the action briefly, as if it is undertaken in a perfunctory manner. More significantly, the narrator states explicitly that "they did not consult Yahweh" (vs. 14). Why is this step not taken? Past episodes have confirmed that trouble is sure to follow when Yahweh is left out of Israel's decisions. Could it be that Israel fears a negative response?

There is also the matter of the covenant itself. Joshua confirms a peaceful relationship between the two peoples (*wayya'as lahem yehoshua' shalom*), and then makes a covenant to let them live (*wayyikrot lahem berit lehayyotam*). The terms of the covenant are intriguing. The verb *hyh* in the Piel (as here) often refers to those who have been spared from death during a massacre or military campaign (Exod 1:17, 18; Num 31:15; Judg 21:14; 2 Kgs 7:4). It is precisely the word Moses uses when he forbids Israel to "spare" anything that breathes (*lo' tehayyeh kol-neshamah*, Deut 20:16). Only the people of Canaan have reason to fear annihilation. Outside Canaan, other rules pertain; there Israel may make peace (*hashlim*) with foreign cities and may subject the inhabitants of those cities to forced labor (Deut 20:10-11). Joshua treats the emissaries as though they do indeed come from a land outside Canaan, but the terms of the treaty respond to and overturn stipulations that apply only to the inhabitants of the land. Why are such stipulations even mentioned?[30]

The covenant with the Gibeonites represents the most serious breach of Yahweh's commandments yet encountered. In the case of Rahab an agreement was also made under an oath which involved the exemption of a family. Now the inhabitants of an entire city and its surrounding villages will be allowed to remain in the land.

The truth is soon revealed. Three days after the covenant is transacted (corresponding to the three days after the oath with

Rahab; 2:22-23), Israel learns that the emissaries who came to them do indeed "live in their midst" (vs. 16). Immediately the Israelites set out for Gibeon, giving the impression that, this time, they will adhere to the words of Moses and put Gibeon under the ban. However, when they reach the city, they do not attack it. This decision causes the "entire assembly" (who do not seem to have been privy to the negotiations) to grumble against their leaders (vs. 18). The grumbling of the people recalls the rebellious grumbling of the previous generation against Moses (Exod 15:24; 16:2, 7; 17:3; Num 14:2, 36; 16:11).[31] However, the situation is now reversed. The Israelites grumble against their leaders not because they are rebellious, but because their leaders are. Perhaps the people, who have been victimized by the last act of rebellion, recognize more clearly than their leaders the dangers involved in running afoul of Yahweh's commandments.

The leaders, who now stand in opposition to the congregation, quickly defuse the people's unrest by presenting the situation as a predicament with no alternatives. They then suggest a compromise.

> All the leaders said to all the congregation, "We swore to them in the name of Yahweh the God of Israel. Now we cannot touch them. This is what we will do with them: we will let them live so that we will not be subject to wrath because of the oath we swore to them." The leaders also said to them, "They are to be spared, but they are to become wood-gatherers and water-carriers for the entire congregation," as the leaders had said to them. (9:19-21)

The leaders' rhetoric is a fine piece of persuasion, carefully laid out and calculated to appease the congregation's outrage. First they clarify the present state of affairs; an action has been undertaken that cannot be undone, and that action precludes the proper execution of the ban. Next they explain that negative consequences will result if the oath is broken. Finally they declare that the Gibeonites must be spared, but with a proviso: the Gibeonites will lose their freedom and become servants of "the entire congregation."

The terms set by the leaders are intended to appease the congregation and mitigate the potentially harmful consequences of the agreement. The designation of the Gibeonites as "wood gatherers and water-carriers" is perhaps a form of punishment and degradation,[32] but the reader is informed that these modifications are implemented "as the princes promised them" (vs. 21b).

The leaders' decision is confirmed by Joshua, who summons the Gibeonites and demands an explanation for their deception. It had been Joshua's decision to make the covenant in the first place. Now he transforms the leaders' decree into a curse and adds a curious modification to the sentence:

> And now, you are cursed. None of you will fail to be a servant; wood-gatherers and water-bearers for the house of my God. (9:23)

Joshua's sentence is even more surprising than the making of the covenant. The wily Gibeonites, a people cursed, will not be separated from Israel but will serve at the very site which signifies the heart of Israel's covenant relationship with Yahweh!

The Gibeonites, however, put in the last word:[33]

> They answered Joshua and said, "Your servants were clearly informed of that which Yahweh your God commanded Moses his servant—to give you the entire land and to exterminate all the inhabitants of the land. We were very afraid for our lives because of you, and so we did this thing. Now look, we are in your hand. Do to us whatever seems good and proper in your opinion." (9:24-25)

One is again struck by the Gibeonites' knowledge and response to Moses' words. They had learned of Yahweh's promise, and, because they evidently believed it, they formed a plan to save themselves. Their final words again take the form of an imperative, urging action on the central issue of the episode. What is the good and proper thing to do here? According to the words of Moses, the good and proper thing is to exterminate all Israel's enemies so that Israel may take possession of the land (Deut 6:18-19).

In Joshua's opinion, however, the good and proper thing to do is to let his decision stand. The decision is a serious one, with far-reaching consequences (vs. 27), for unlike Rahab and her family, who were consigned to a place outside the camp, the Gibeonites are integrated into community and cultus. The narrator does not conceal the fact that the responsibility for the covenant and the exemption of the Gibeonites lies ultimately with Joshua.

> And that is what he did to them. He delivered them from the hands of the Israelites and did not execute them. (9:26)

To "deliver from the hand of" most often expresses Yahweh's activity with reference to Israel (Judg 6:9; 9:17; 1 Sam 4:8; 7:3; 10:18; 12:11; 14:48; 17:37; Ezra 8:31). In sparing the Gibeonites, Joshua stands with the cursed inhabitants of the land against those who would adhere to Yahweh's commands and exterminate them.

The story of the Gibeonite covenant deconstructs the plot of obedient Israel, so recently affirmed by the victory over Ai and the ceremony at Mounts Ebal and Gerizim. As in the stories involving Rahab and Achan, an ominous mood is created by narrating the story against the backdrop of another, threatening text. In this case, the story of forbidden covenant-making is related by appropriating themes and motifs of Moses' speech during the covenant renewal on the plains of Moab (Deut 29:1-29).

The covenant renewal related in Deuteronomy 29 contains three elements: an admonition to keep the covenant in response to God's gracious deeds, a declaration of God's willingness to make the covenant, and a warning that God will destroy Israel if it does not abide by the terms of the covenant (Polzin 1980: 118). A striking number of literary allusions link the episode at Gibeon with Moses' words on the plains of Moab. These allusions prompt the reader to recall that covenant renewal, and thus they evoke the grid of obedience while telling the story of a serious transgression. The connections are all the more striking when one remembers that the generation which had affirmed the covenant in Moab is the same one that now makes a covenant with Gibeon. Failure and disobedience lie in the background as the episode develops.

Two vivid images are taken from the Deuteronomic context. The first is connected to the Gibeonites and their appearance. Moses had called Israel to remember what Yahweh had done for them, particularly the signs they had seen Yahweh perform in Egypt. Furthermore, during the entire time that they had wandered in the wilderness, their clothing and sandals had not worn out, nor did they consume any bread or fermented drink (Deut 29:4-5). However, Moses remarked, Yahweh had not given "a heart to know, eyes to see, and ears to hear until this very day" (Deut 29:3).

The Gibeonites, however, hear and understand what Yahweh has done at Jericho, Ai, and in the Transjordan, and they know what Yahweh has promised to Israel (Josh 9:3, 9, 24). The ruse which they devise is appropriately ironic: worn-out clothing, patched sandals, stale bread, and old wineskins. They in fact look like Israel would have looked had it not been for Yahweh. Furthermore, they approach Israel as Israel had once approached Sihon, with an offer of peace (*hashlim*; Deut 2:26-31).[34]

The second connection with Deuteronomy 29 is made through the sentence passed by Joshua and the leaders of Israel once the ruse is discovered. Upon discovering the emissaries' true identity, Joshua and the Israelite leaders decree that the Gibeonites will be "wood-gatherers and water-carriers" for Israel. The phrase occurs in but one other context.

> All of you are standing before Yahweh your God today: your chieftains and tribes, your elders and officials, and every man of Israel, as well as your children and women, and the sojourner who lives within your camps—from your wood-gatherer to your water bearer. (Deut 29:9-10)

In a sense, the covenant with Gibeon has been foreshadowed by that made in Moab. And, as the narrator of Joshua reminds us, the Gibeonites remain within Israel "to this day" (Josh 9:26).

By using these images to connect the two passages, the narrator brings Moses' words on the previous occasion into the present scenario. They are singularly appropriate. Moses had admonished the people not to turn away to worship other gods (Deut 29:15-18) and warned Israel not to disregard the words of the oath which had confirmed the covenant.

> When that person hears the words of this oath and blesses themselves, saying, "All is well with me. I will indeed walk stubbornly" so that both watered and dry land vanish, I will not be willing to forgive him. Then the wrath and jealousy of Yahweh will smolder against that person, and every curse written in this book will come to rest on them. Yahweh will separate that person from all the tribes of Israel for calamity according to all the curses of the covenant, written in this book of instruction. (Deut 29:19-20)

Moses' warnings of Yahweh's wrath and jealousy are particularly ominous as Israel negotiates with Gibeon. Achan has just been "separated" from the tribes of Israel for his transgression, and Israel as a whole has experienced the burning anger of Yahweh (Josh 7:1, 26; Deut 29:23, 27). According to Moses, breaking the covenant will lead to the expulsion of Israel from the land (Deut 29:22-28), and, ironically, Moses predicts that the "foreigners who come from distant lands" will be among those who will see the catastrophes which Yahweh will bring (Deut 29:22). By shaping the story of the Gibeonite emissaries according to this Deuteronomic text, the narrative expresses the opposing plot of disobedience and once again disrupts the movement toward fulfillment.

Joshua's curse, along with his decision to give the Gibeonites a place within Israel, ostensibly resolves the problem of the covenant with Gibeon. In so doing it represses the sense of Israel's disobedience once again. Even so, it appears to work. When the kings of the region learn that Gibeon has "made peace" (hashlim) with Joshua (Josh 10:1, 4), they join together to make war against Gibeon (10:5). This might seem to be a providential solution to Israel's problem. That is, although they can initiate no hostilities towards Gibeon because of the oath, the other kings may do the job for them. Israel may yet be free of Gibeon! But when the Gibeonites call for help, Joshua responds with crack troops.

Even more surprising is Yahweh's complicity in the decision to save Gibeon. When Joshua marches to aid Gibeon against the five Amorite kings, Yahweh encourages him (10:8) and even joins in the battle to fight for Israel (10:14b)! The narrator goes to some lengths to inform the reader that Yahweh is indeed with Israel again. In a climactic twist of the plot, for example, the narrator exclaims that now even Yahweh "obeys" (shama‘) Joshua (10:14), pelting the Amorites with hail and stopping the movement of both sun and moon to Israel's benefit. The account of the victory at Gibeon is followed by a repetitive summary of more successes in southern Canaan. Yahweh's exaggerated response (and the narrator's report of divine warring), along with the repeated accounts of additional victories, counters the disruption of the Gibeonite treaty. Israel's disobedience, and the threat it elicits, is once more repressed, and the narrative continues toward fulfillment.

The story of the northern campaign is related briefly (11:1-15), condensing the events of a long period of real time into a relatively small space of text. As noted previously, the summary of the campaign displays, in miniature, the dynamic which shapes the story of Israel's initial campaigns in Canaan. The first section of the book, nevertheless, concludes on a strongly positive note. A series of victory reports is presented, first in the form of a narrative summary of victories in Canaan (11:16-23) and then in the form of a list of the defeated kings of the land (12:9-24). The catalogue of successes implicitly affirms that the story is on track toward the desired end—at least for the time being.

Thus the first segment of the book ends with repeated assertions of Israel's success in Canaan and looks forward to the apportionment of the land among the tribes (11:23b). The land has rest from warfare (11:23c), and the kings of the land have been subdued (12:9-24). But there is more to the story than this. The land has yet to be divided and settled. In effect, the promise of possession is still unfulfilled.

As the narrative moves on to relate the next part of the story, issues of obedience and disobedience are subsumed by a different set of plots—those having to do with integrity and fragmentation. The patterns of obedience and disobedience are still apparent—there are references to commands and rituals (13:6; 14:2, 5; 17:4; 18:3-10)—but in comparison to the plots of integrity and fragmentation, they have only a peripheral part in shaping the narrative.

THE INTERACTION OF PLOTS

As we have seen, the story of the possession of the promised land begins by elaborating the conditions that must be met in order to achieve success. Joshua must be obedient to Moses (and thus to Yahweh) and Israel must be obedient to Yahweh. The point is repeatedly made: obedience will lead to fulfillment, disobedience will result in an unsatisfactory and premature ending. Events demonstrating Israel's obedience are linked together into a pattern that points toward Israel's final victory and settlement in the land. This pattern constitutes a plot, discernable through the recurring motifs of Israel's obedience and fidelity to Yahweh.

However, as soon as the Israelites cross the Jordan into Canaan, they commit a serious breach of conduct. The oath with Rahab introduces an opposing plot—a plot of disobedience—which subverts the symbols of obedience (oath, covenant, and ban) and tells the story differently. In this version, both Joshua and Israel are bested by the peoples of the land, who lead them to transgress the covenant made with Yahweh. The threatening aspects of these episodes are accentuated by subtle allusions to previous disruptive events, which echo through the telling of the stories.

The two conflicting plot lines compete and move the text along, mirroring the contest between Israel and Canaan. Israel walks in obedience to Yahweh but is repeatedly drawn away from obedience by contact with Canaan (whether its people or its treasures). These instances of disobedience threaten to abort the drive toward fulfillment initiated at the beginning, and require a resolution so that the narrative can continue on course. However, in each case the resolution fails to dissipate the threat completely: Rahab, Achan, and the Gibeonites all remain with Israel ("to this day," 6:25; 7:26; 9:27). The narrative thus exhibits the "working out" of the energies of disobedience through a repetitive pattern that shapes the story of Israel's encounters with the inhabitants of the land.

This working out is undertaken with a high level of ambivalence, which is evident in the configuration of events as well as in their ordering. The stories of Rahab and the Gibeonites are told in ways that focus on Israel's disobedience but that also elicit sympathy. Rahab and the Gibeonites both acclaim Yahweh's deeds, appearing as allies as well as opponents. The reader may thus experience a certain satisfaction when they are spared, even though their salvation threatens the fulfillment of the story as a whole. Achan's willing compliance and declaration of faith also elicit sympathy, even though his transgression threatens to undo the entire program. When he and his entire family are executed, Yahweh turns from his anger. But how much satisfaction is gained by the execution of a repentant Israelite?

A characteristic of textual energy is that it "should always be on the verge of premature discharge, of short-circuit" (Brooks 1984:108). The possibility of an undesirable end is present throughout the story, and always at the point where desire has been recently affirmed. In Joshua 1-12, the reader encounters a number of serious instances of disobedience to the commandments of Moses. Each of these instances threatens Israel's fulfillment of the promises articulated at the beginning of the book. In every case, the threats are, at least superficially, resolved, and the image of an obedient Israel is restored. The story oscillates between obedience and disobedience, and in the process creates a sense of ambiguity and tension about the fulfillment of the promise.

5

INTEGRITY
AND
FRAGMENTATION

Although the obedience of Israel is the dominant configurational agenda in Joshua 1-12, the desire for integrity exerts a considerable influence on the way these episodes are rendered. The working out of this plot line is expressed in catalogues of Israel's victories (as in 10:28-42 or 12:9-24), declarations of victory (6:16; 8:1-2; 11:6), reports that Israel acts as a unit (1:2; 3:1; 5:5; 8:15, 21; 10:29), assertions that Yahweh is with Israel (1:5,9; 6:2-5; 8:1-2, 18; 10:8, 11-13, 25; 11:6, 20), and reports that "no one remained" (8:22; 10:28, 40; 11:8, 14). In the account of the Jordan crossing (3:1-4:24), furthermore, the desire for integrity—and its contest with fragmentation—is apparent.

ENTRY INTO THE LAND

The crossing is represented in terms of totality. It is undertaken by "all Israel" (3:1, 7, 17; 4:14), "the entire nation" (3:17; 4:1, 11). Even the eastern tribes, who have chosen to settle outside the promised land, are to be included, so that the event can be experienced by the nation as a whole. Israel must enter the land as a unit, even if it should later segment so that some may return to the Transjordan.

This impulse to render the episode in comprehensive terms can also be detected in the unique name given to the Ark of the

Covenant. Here it is called the "Ark of the Covenant of the Lord of All the Land" (3:11,13). Israel follows the Ark in and through the Jordan, following a command/response format that illustrates a complete concordance between Yahweh, Joshua and Israel (4:10).

The crossing itself is an event highly symbolic of Israel's transformation from a disordered to an ordered people. The narration of the event has a mythic quality, and its etiological elements in particular sanction and reinforce the symbolic network which constitutes Israel's perception of reality. By crossing the Jordan, Israel moves from wilderness—the place of chaos—to the promised land—the place of order.

> In and through the myth, "land" becomes a cipher for a total social order. The move into the land is nothing short of that creative change from chaos to ordered cosmos. (Thompson 1981:356)[1]

By crossing the Jordan, Israel enters a bounded place and leaves the vast expanse of the wilderness. The transformation is made possible by Yahweh, "frame-maker, boundary-keeper and master of transformations" (Thompson 1981:357), who, represented by the Ark, stands between chaos and ordered existence. The narrative thus accentuates the liturgical elements of the episode in order to focus the reader's attention on the symbolic significance of the boundary being traversed.[2] The priests, who oversee Israel's maintenance and traversing of boundaries, stand, appropriately, in the middle of the border-region to mediate journey of the entire people from wilderness to promised land. Extensive preparations are undertaken to ensure that the crossing is made in an orderly and integrated manner (3:1-13), and this is precisely what is done. Throughout the episode, the ostensive plot depicts the Jordan crossing in terms of wholes and boundaries. Thus Israel as a people has crossed over into a new, ordered existence with Yahweh (who confirms the transformation with a miraculous stoppage of the water).

Yet this sense of integrity is violated by the muddled way in which the narrative relates Israel's crossing. In fact, nowhere else in Joshua does the narrative seem in such disarray.

Scholars have long noted the disjointed structure, inconsistencies, and overlapping that characterize the narration at this point. The sequence of events within the episode is unclear, and the crossing itself seems to be narrated twice (3:14-4:1; 4:10-18).[3]

Nowhere is the confusion more apparent than in the erection of the twelve stones. A command to select one man from each tribe appears abruptly in the midst of Joshua's directions for the crossing (3:12). The command is clarified in 4:7; the twelve are commanded to take stones from the Jordan and set them up as a memorial. It is executed when the men take stones from the Jordan and set them up in the camp (vs. 8). However, the next report seems to indicate that Joshua set up twelve stones in the middle of the Jordan, at the place where the priest stood with the Ark of the Covenant (vs. 9). Finally, the reader is told that Joshua erected the stones taken from the Jordan at Gilgal (4:20), which is now designated as the site of the Israelite camp (4:19). How many events does the narrative refer to, one or many? And where is the memorial? at Gilgal? in the middle of the Jordan?

More significant is the sense that, textually speaking, the Jordan is crossed not once but many times. Instead of presenting a straightforward account of the crossing, the narrator seems to take the reader back and forth across the Jordan. Israel begins in the Transjordan, and crosses proleptically through the instructions given by Joshua (presented in great detail; 3:9-13). The crossing event is then related in its entirety, beginning in the Israelite camp (3:14), and concluding with the remark that "all Israel crossed on dry land until all the people had finished crossing the Jordan" (3:17). The next segment begins at the same place (4:1), but then returns to the Jordan, where the establishment of the stone memorial is repeatedly recounted (4:8-10).

The entire account begins again in 4:10-13, which actually relates a series of crossings: by "the entire people" (vs. 10b), by the priests (vs. 11), and the eastern tribes (who cross before the rest of Israel; vs. 12). The conclusion of the episode is marked by a return to the priests, whose exit from the Jordan causes the water to flow once more (4:18).

The many textual crossings of the Jordan inject ambiguity into the telling of an episode that is of critical importance. Rather than simply relating the crossing, the account creates an impression of disorientation. The geographical location and chronological sequence are jumbled many times. This sense of dislocation continues in a summary statement that connects the Jordan crossing with the circumcision ceremony at Gibeath Haaraloth. Here the narrator draws attention back to the Transjordanian perspective by explicitly describing "the other side of the Jordan" as "the west side."

> When all the kings of the Amorites on the other side of the Jordan—the west side—and all the kings of the Canaanites near the sea heard that Yahweh had dried up the water of the Jordan before the Israelites until they crossed over, their hearts melted and they were demoralized before the Israelites. (5:1)

The crossing is then recounted a final time, now from the perspective of the kings in Canaan. Thus, although Israel has already crossed the Jordan, the text places the reader back in the Transjordan. This move is accomplished by the placement of the Amorite kings on the other side of the Jordan, and the narrator calls attention to the shift of perspective by emphasizing that, in this context, "the other side" is to be understood as the land west of the Jordan.[4] The movement back and forth across the Jordan blurs its function as a boundary. Furthermore, the narrative continues to be ambiguous about what constitutes "the other side" of the Jordan, at some points indicating Cisjordan (5:1; 9:1; 12:7; 22:7) and at others Transjordan (1:14; 2:10; 7:7; 12:1; 13:8). The constant shift in perspective creates the sense that "Israel" is to be located on both sides of the Jordan, and compromises the Jordan's status as a boundary which defines Israel and the promised land (a situation underscored by the attention and preeminence afforded to the eastern tribes during the episode; 4:12-13).

Does the narrative's vacillation between the two banks of the boundary suggest a vacillation in Israel's resolve? It is perhaps significant that the crossing of the Jordan connects the present generation with that of the Exodus generation (4:23). Both generations have participated in a crossing and share experiences of deliverance and wonder. Will they share experiences of failure as well?

In the Jordan crossing, the reader encounters an apparently climactic event in which a unified Israel acts in complete accord with Yahweh. Yet the presentation is incoherent and incongruous, creating a sense of ambiguity and disorientation rather than confidence and assurance. The episode reaches its conclusion, not by a straightforward and purposeful advance, but by a convoluted path filled with detours and repetitions. Beneath the surface of the text the interacting patterns of integrity and fragmentation play out their contest to push the narrative towards disparate conclusions.

The interaction of these textual drives finally surfaces, however, when the story moves from entry into the land (2-12) to its definition and possession (13-21).

THE LAND POSSESSED AND NOT POSSESSED

The first section of the book of Joshua concludes with expansive reports of Israel's comprehensive success in subjugating the promised land. The impression of total victory is created by the narrator's summary in 11:16-23 and is reinforced by the impressive catalogue of kings which Joshua and the Israelites have defeated (12:7-24). The information in 12:1-24 further widens the scope to summarize all Israelite conquests, both in the Transjordan and in Canaan, thus linking the recent victories with those related by Moses (Deut 2:24-3:11). Israel's successful possession of the Transjordanian lands is reviewed in familiar terms (vss. 1-6), beginning with a programmatic introduction: "These are the kings of the land which the Israelites attacked and took possession of" (vs. 1). The catalogue of the defeated Canaanite kings is introduced in similar fashion (vss. 7-8), with one important exception. The summary begins with another declaration: "These are the kings of the land which Joshua and the Israelites attacked." But there is a notable absence; the possession of the land is not mentioned. This absence is significant, because possession of the land confirms fulfillment. Possession is the end toward which the entire story moves (1:11). The summary in 12:1-24 therefore affirms Israel's victories but also points out the difference between the campaigns in Transjordan and in Canaan. Despite its successes, Israel has not yet been able to take possession of Canaan as it has the kingdoms of Sihon and Og (cf. Deut 3:12, 20).

It is also significant that the next major section, which relates the allocation and definition of tribal territories (Josh 13-21), begins with a description of the large areas of land yet to be possessed (13:1-7). The information is presented as an exhortation by Yahweh, which marks a new beginning and defines the central concern of the corpus which follows.[5] The exhortation is a private communication to Joshua. It is presumably long after the events in 1-12, for Joshua has "grown old and well-advanced in days" (13:1a). Yahweh's words on this occasion echo those of the initial exhortation to Joshua (1:1-9). Once again Yahweh speaks of the task which lies ahead of Israel (13:1; 1:2), defines the extent of land to be taken (13:2-5; 1:3-4), and offers promises of victory (13:6-7; 1:6-9).

These opening words from Yahweh correspond to the words with which Moses introduced his description of tribal territories in Transjordan (Deut 3:12-20) and the comparison again accentuates the difference between the two contexts. In the case of the Transjordan, a description of what had been possessed preceded the allocation of territory. In the case of Joshua, however, possession is rendered in negative terms, thus highlighting Israel's failures rather than its successes. The focus becomes non-possession, and thus non-fulfillment.[6]

The notice of land remaining also contrasts with the optimism reflected in the exhortations which began the book (1:2-9). At that time, Yahweh had spoken expansively of Israel's potential for fulfillment ("every place," "all the land of the Hittites," etc.). Now, however, Yahweh's expansive language describes the vast incompleteness of Israel's task ("all" the regions of the Philistines, and "all" the Geshurites, "all" the land of the Canaanites, "all" the Lebanon, "all" the inhabitants of the mountainous country). Yahweh's description of the land no longer functions to encourage Israel of its potential for success but accentuates Israel's failure. The focus is not on what Israel has successfully possessed but on what it has failed to possess.

Yahweh has also become less expansive in the promises he makes to Israel. Earlier, Yahweh had promised to dispossess the inhabitants of the land (Deut 9:1-4) and to be with Israel wherever it chose to go (Josh 1:3a, 9b). However, Yahweh's promises are now more restrictive; promises for divine aid seem to extend only to Israel's acquisition of the Sidonian land (13:6).

The extensive affirmation of Israel's fulfillment in 11:16-12:24 thus abruptly gives way to a more negative assessment (13:1-7), manifesting the potential for failure and disintegration. The negative is, in turn, countered by another positive, as the text returns a final time to the paradigmatic story of success embodied in the Transjordanian conquests (Israel took possession of "the entire kingdoms" of Sihon and Og; 13:8-33). In so doing, the images of the land not taken are again sublimated by the image of land completely possessed.

Two plots push the narrative in contrary directions. The plot of integrity drives toward the desired end of fulfillment and rest in the land. In what follows, this plot is marked by a pronounced emphasis on the definition and maintenance of boundaries. The boundaries of the promised land demarcate Israel from other peoples, and the allotment of territories to the individual tribes structures Israel's life as a people. The establishment of boundaries thus represents an organization of the social order, and, in an even broader sense, a management of reality.[7]

A fragmenting counter-plot, however, points to a different end—an end in which Israel fails to possess all the land Yahweh has promised. This plot is marked by disruptive notes about the presence of non-Israelite peoples within the borders of Israel and by the blurring of the very boundaries which are intended to organize and define Israel's life in the land. The disruptions of this fragmenting counter-plot are apparent throughout Joshua 13-21.

THE LAND IN THE TRANSJORDAN

After Yahweh's introductory comments to Joshua (13:1-7), the following material can be divided into four main sections, each relating a different aspect of Israel's possession of the land. The first, 13:8-33, describes the tribal areas to be possessed by the eastern tribes and repeats once more the victories gained in that region. The following section, 14:1-17:18, concerns the major tribes of Joseph and Judah. The assignment of territory to the remaining seven tribes is the subject of the third section, 18:1-51. Finally, there are two segments concerning people of marginal status in Israel (those unaffected by boundaries): manslayers and Levites, 20:1-21:42.

The apportionment of land in the Transjordan (13:8-33) is divided into two subsections. The first (vss. 8-14) describes the general extent of Transjordanian land occupied by Israel, while the second (vss. 15-32) defines the specific territories assigned to Reuben, Gad, and the half-tribe of Manasseh. The account is notable not only for its specificity but also for its comprehensiveness. Once again, the key term *kol* ("all") appears repeatedly (twelve times in all) to describe the extent of territory taken in the Transjordan (vss. 9, 10, 11 [x2], 12, 16, 17, 21 [x2], 25, 30 [x2]). Reports of other victories are included as well, specifically Israel's triumph over the Midianite chieftains and the prophet Balaam (vss. 21-22).

By presenting the Transjordanian apportionments in these terms, the narrator not only establishes a pattern of organization (which the reader will expect in the division of the Cisjordanian lands as well) but also effectively represses the fragmentation and incompleteness which has disrupted the text in 13:1-7. The narrator explicitly affirms that the territory east of the Jordan has been taken (*laqah*) by the tribes of Reuben, Gad, and half-Manasseh. The verb *laqah* is also used to summarize Joshua's comprehensive success in Canaan ("Joshua took the entire land"; 11:16, 23). Its use in this context thus brings the accounts of victories in the Transjordan together with those in Canaan. The textual breach, caused by the report of land not possessed, is thereby ostensibly closed, and the story regains a sense of totality and success.

However, a few fissures still remain. First, the figure of Moses is prominent, reminding the reader that the successes being recounted occurred in a previous era. Coming as it does, immediately after Yahweh's speech to Joshua, Moses' reappearance forces a contrast between past and present. In the Mosaic phase of the occupation, the tribes enjoyed complete success and took all the land which Yahweh gave (13:8, 12, 32). Now, under Joshua, Israel enjoys only partial success.

Second, the review of Israel's Transjordanian possessions contains a curious aside.

> But the Israelites did not dispossess the Geshurites or the Maacathites. Geshur and Maacah dwell in the midst of Israel to this day. (13:13)

The report seems irrelevant at first. The regions of Geshur and Maacah are nowhere assigned to any of the tribes, nor are they included in the Transjordanian land granted by Moses. Of course Israel did not dispossess them! They were not, after all, one of Israel's objectives (unless the reader is to assume that they were encompassed within Og's domain, which seems unlikely).

The cryptic reference to Geshur and Maacah is nonetheless a significant disruption. First, it intimates that, during a later period, Israel did try to occupy the region, but with only partial success (thus pointing to future failures). Second, the report reminds the reader of other peoples within the Promised Land—the Rahabites and Gibeonites, who also live "among the Israelites to this day" (6:25; 9:27). Finally, the report establishes a disconcerting precedent, one that foreshadows more serious instances of peoples not dispossessed. It seems that, even in this account of comprehensive success, the integrity of Israel in the land is ambiguous.

JUDAH AND JOSEPH

The next major block of material (14:1-17:18) concerns the acquisition of the territories settled by the tribes of Judah and Joseph. After a general introduction (14:1-5), the narrative moves to report the areas assigned to Judah (14:6-15:63) and to Ephraim and half-Manasseh (16:1-17:18). The boundary and city lists in this section are framed by two mini-narratives which relate the efforts of certain groups to take possession of their territory—Caleb (14:6-15) and the people of Joseph (17:15-18). The lists themselves are separated by two short vignettes which relate the inheritance of land by women—Achsah (15:13-19) and Zelophehad's daughters (17:3-6).

The narrator begins this section by presenting a story of unmitigated success and obedience. Caleb, a tribal leader of Judah (Num 13:6; 34:19), is a paradigm of faith and blessing, representing all that Israel is to be.[8] His monologue (14:6b-12) repeats the motifs of blessing, obedience, and the promise of the land. Caleb remembers the words of Moses (vs. 6), and aggressively seeks the land promised to him on oath (vs. 9a). He has spoken in truth (vs. 7) and has exercised a singular devotion to Yahweh (vs. 9c), even when others demurred (vs. 8). Though an old man, his speech is animated with energy and urgency, and he practically demands the very territory which appears most difficult to take (vs. 12). Caleb's monologue represents the response that Israel as a whole has been expected to offer. He is an eager partner with Yahweh in dispossessing giants and conquering strongholds.

By beginning this section with a heroic rendering of the story of Caleb, the narrative reaffirms the plot of a robust Israel which dispossesses the land's inhabitants. The promise of land given to Caleb (vs. 9b; Deut 1:36) is strongly reminiscent of that given to Israel through Joshua (1:3). Caleb is thus a metaphor for Israel. Through his story, the narrator affirms an Israel that faithfully remembers and responds to Yahweh's promises. As with Caleb in particular, so with Israel as a whole.

The description of Judah's territory follows and is appropriately expansive. Its borders are outlined with meticulous detail (15:1-11) and encompass an impressive catalogue of cities, carefully organized according to geographical area (15:20-62). The narrative devotes more textual space to the tracing of Judah's territory than it does to any other tribe; in effect, Judah possesses a great deal of textual "territory" relative to the other tribes. The narrator, by this device, echoes the homogeneity and extent of Judah's actual territory in relation to that of other tribes. Judah—Caleb's tribe—acquires an extensive and well-ordered territory.

Caleb's story continues after the borders of Judah are elaborated (15:13-19). Picking up where the story left off, the narrator recounts the taking of Hebron and Debir and adds to this account the story of Caleb's daughter Achsah. The insertion of the rest of the story, at this point, is puzzling. Why has the story been split? And why has the latter part been inserted between the description of borders and the list of cities? One strong possibility is that the two segments of the story mirror the promise-fulfillment program of the book as a whole. The first segment focuses on the promise of land made to Caleb, while the second relates its fulfillment in the taking of Hebron and Debir. By dividing Caleb's story and entwining it with the description of Judahite possessions, the narrator is able to reinforce the perception that Judah is successful in taking possession of the territory promised and allotted to it. Caleb responded to the promise and saw its fulfillment, and so, we are led to assume, did Caleb's tribe.

There is, however, a curious postscript to the account of Judah's acquisitions.

> The Judahites were unable to dispossess the Jebusites who lived in Jerusalem. The Jebusites dwell with the Judahites, in Jerusalem, to this day. (15:63)

As with the note that the eastern tribes did not dispossess the inhabitants of Geshur and Maacah, the comment here is noteworthy because it seems unnecessary. Jerusalem is not situated within the territory allotted to Judah, and yet the narrator informs the reader that the people of Jerusalem live among the people of Judah "to this day." The comment, nonetheless, signifies a disruption, intimating a future breakdown of boundaries (Judahites living in the area of Jerusalem, outside the prescribed borders), and repeating the threatening image of non-Israelites within Israel. The notice is all the more damaging since it occurs at the end of the account, thereby frustrating the drive for closure and leaving a gap in the otherwise well-defined parameters of the text. The note lies outside the borders of text, just as Jerusalem lies outside the boundary of Judah, but it nonetheless intimates an association between Jerusalem and Judah which signals a disintegration in tribal and territorial integrity.

There are other ambiguities. For example, the reader was previously informed that Joshua, not Caleb, took Hebron and Debir (10:36-39) and destroyed the Anakim (11:21). The brief vignette about Achsah is also noteworthy. Achsah is given to Othniel as a prize for taking Debir.

> When she arrived, she urged him to ask her father for a field. She dismounted from the donkey, and Caleb said, "What's the matter?"
> She said, "Give me a blessing. Since you have given me land in the Negeb, give me springs of water."
> So he gave her the upper and lower springs. (15:18-19)

The vignette is marked by brevity, communicating a rapid sequence of events which are, on the whole, dictated by Achsah. The verbs which describe the action precipitated by her evoke both power and humor. Upon her arrival (presumably at Othniel's encampment), she immediately sets about the task of persuading her new husband to acquire part of her father's land. The force of her persuasion is intimated by the verb *tesitehu* ("incited"), as well as by the unusual *plene* writing of the infinitival *holem* in *lish'ol* ("to ask"). Rendered this way, *lish'ol* puns on "Sheol," the Hebrew term for the grave. Othniel is silent, and, we may assume, compliant.

Achsah is able to acquire the springs necessary to guarantee the productiveness of her land. It is clear that she considers the land her own; there is no mention of her husband in the demand she makes of Caleb ("Give me a blessing. Since you have given me land in the Negeb, give me springs of water."). Achsah is like her ancestor Jacob, demanding a blessing and refusing to be put off. But she is even more like Rahab. Confronting the men of Israel, she demands and receives from them a place within the land. Using only the power of her words, she bests the heroes of Judah and gets what she wants. Achsah acquires. Caleb acquiesces.

The description of Judah's acquisitions evokes a sense of integrity (through the tribe's well-defined and homogenous boundaries) and of zeal (through stories portraying the faithfulness and success of Caleb and his family). The extensive textual material devoted to Judah affirms the fulfillment of the land promise, even as it raises troubling ambiguities.

The account of the Joseph tribes, which follows that of Judah (16:1-17:18), presents the obverse of this construct. Like the previous account, it is divided into sections: a general summary (16:1-4), the delineation of the territory of Ephraim (16:5-10), reports of heroes (both men and women; 17:1-6), the delineation of the territory of Manasseh (17:7-13), and an account of settlement (17:14-18). However, while the narrator presented Judah's acquisitions in holistic terms, Joseph's situation appears fragmented and uncertain.

The status of the descendants of Joseph is ambivalent from the beginning. They receive one allotment (16:1), as if they constitute one tribe, yet they are recognized as two distinct tribal units (Manasseh and Ephraim; 14:4a). This ambiguity is reinforced by the narrative framework, which puts material concerning "Joseph" at the sides of the frame (16:1-4; 17:14-18) and recounts the allotments of the Manasseh and Ephraim in the intervening text. In addition, one of the tribes, Manasseh, is further divided. Part of the tribe receives an allotment across the Jordan, while the remainder is assigned territory in the promised land (17:1-2).

The descriptions of the territories of Ephraim and Manasseh correspond to the account of Judah's territory in 15:1-63. Both begin with the delineation of tribal boundaries (16:5-8; 17:7-10), which define the areas as units. However, while the description of Judah's borders is related with precision and detail, those of Ephraim and Manasseh are fragmentary, take up much less textual space, and present numerous topographical difficulties. The integrity of Judah's territory is thus contrasted with the broken contours of the land settled by the Joseph tribes.[9]

Appended to each description of boundaries is a note which relates the cities assigned to each tribe.

The cities separated out for the Ephraimites were within the inheritance of the Manassites, all the cities and their villages. (16:9)

Manasseh had within Issachar and Asher, Beth-Shean, Ibleam, the inhabitants of Dor and En-Dor, Taanach, and Megiddo, along with their dependencies; the three of Napheth. (17:11)

The contrast with Judah is once again striking. Where settlements of Judah are catalogued in great detail and are neatly organized into districts, the only Ephraimite cities mentioned are not even located within Ephraim, but lie within the territory of Manasseh. And not one of the cities is named! Likewise, there is no report of cities within Manasseh; the cities listed for Manasseh lie outside its borders. Such reports render the function of the boundaries (however fragmentary they might be) virtually meaningless. Ephraim and Manasseh are mixed together, and Manasseh commingles with Issachar and Asher.

Finally, the descriptions of Ephraim and Manasseh both conclude with reports of areas not taken.

They did not dispossess the Canaanites who dwell in Gezer. The Canaanites dwell in the midst of Ephraim to this day, and they have been put to forced labor. (16:10)

The Manassites were not able to dispossess these cities. The Canaanites were determined to dwell in this land. When the Israelites grew strong, they put the Canaanites to forced labor. But they never did dispossess them. (17:12)

As in the other aspects of the presentation, these reports correspond to the concluding comments made concerning Judah (15:63). However, in the case of Judah, the disruption caused by the notice of failure to take Jerusalem was muted by the fact that the city was not located within the boundaries of Judah in the first place. In the case of Ephraim and Manasseh, however, the reports signify a more severe disruption and further undercut the construction of territorial homogeneity. There are gaps *within* the borders of these two tribes, just as there are gaps *in* the borders. Furthermore, contrary to the commandments of Moses, the land's inhabitants are not exterminated but are merely subjected to servitude. The situation continues "to this day," thus adding the Canaanites at Gezer and in Manasseh to the growing list of failures and exceptions. The territorial descriptions of Ephraim and Manasseh therefore do not close properly, and leave the reader with a sense of territorial confusion rather than territorial integrity.

Between descriptions of the borders of Ephraim and Manasseh there is a brief narrative section addressing matters of inheritance. This time the recipients of territory are the daughters of Zelophehad (17:1-6), who are the Josephite counterparts of Achsah of Judah. They are women who demand and receive a place for themselves within the allotted land. In addition to these heroines, it seems that Manasseh has heroes of its own as well; the clan of Machir is warlike and receives for itself both Gilead and Bashan (17:1).

The inclusion of information concerning the sons of Machir and the daughters of Zelophehad would seem to serve the same affirmative function in the context of Joseph's account as the mention of Caleb and Achsah did for Judah. There is, however, one crucial difference between the women and heroes of Judah and those of Manasseh. Manasseh's women, along with its heroes, live on the other side of the Jordan, where the land promise has been fulfilled. They live apart from those of their tribe who live in the promised land. Their status therefore not only reiterates the fragmented condition of Manasseh (and Israel as a whole) but accentuates again the contrasting situations developing on the respective sides of the Jordan. Manasseh in the Transjordan actively possesses its inheritance. For the remainder of Manasseh within the promised land, on the other hand, there is no one worthy of note.

The description of Joseph's territories concludes with a report of the tribes' quest for more territory in the land of the Perizzites and Rephaim (17:14-18). The report is presented at the conclusion in order to complement the story of Caleb's quest for land narrated at the beginning (14:6-15). Taken together, these two episodes act as frames for the body of material reporting the territories of Israel's major tribes in Canaan. The opening story of Caleb is narrated in heroic terms and thus reasserts the plot of integrity and success; Caleb is courageous, faithful, and zealous, fearing neither giants nor walls. The concluding story of the Josephites, however, is in many ways the antithesis of Caleb's, conveying trepidation, contentiousness, and failure.

Joshua's encounter with the Josephites is an ironic repetition of his encounter with Caleb.[10] Whereas Caleb's request for land constituted a confession of faith, the Josephites' request comes in the form of a complaint. They are discontented with what they have been given and insist that they should receive more than one allotment, pointing to their great numbers as evidence of divine blessing (vs. 14).

The contrast with Caleb is especially pointed as the Josephites press for a place that will be easy to settle. Caleb had asked for hill country but was given a city (14:12a). The Josephites are given hill country and refuse to take the cities. Caleb had been eager to dispossess giants, and was not intimidated by fortified cities. The Josephites face giants (the Rephaim; cf. Deut 3:11) and fortified cities as well, but respond very differently (vss. 15-16). When Joshua responds to their petition by instructing them to clear land in the region of the Perizzites and Rephaim, they complain further. No confident declarations here!

The reason why the Josephites' allotment is too small is that they have confined themselves to the hill country and have not taken the choice land in the plain and Jezreel for fear of the Canaanites.

> The Josephites said, "The hill country is not enough for us, and all the Canaanites who live in the valley region of Beth-Shean and its settlements, and in the Jezreel valley, have iron chariots." (17:16)

Caleb proclaimed that, with Yahweh's help, he could dispossess those who inhabited the fortified cities. Now Joshua must exhort the Josephites, both Ephraim and Manasseh, to dispossess the cities of the plain and valley.

> You are a numerous people, and you have great power. You shall not have just one allotment. You shall have the hill country, even though it is wooded. You will clear it, and you shall have it as far as it goes. You must, indeed, dispossess the

Canaanites, even though they have iron chariots and are strong. (17:17b-18)[11]

Joshua's exhortation brings the stories of Judah and Joseph to an unsettling end. This section began with Caleb's confident assertions and successes, along with the assurance of cessation of warfare (14:15b). But there is no such closure at the end. The reader is not told of the response of the Joseph tribes and knows only that these areas will be taken at a later time (16:10; 17:12). Neither bold nor successful, the Josephites are timid and complaining. The plot of integrity, so important to the attainment of fulfillment, has been supplanted by a plot of fragmentation pointing to an increasingly uncertain conclusion.

THE SEVEN REMAINING TRIBES

The report of an assembly at Shiloh (18:1) marks the beginning of a new unit and reaffirms Israel's homogeneity. The failures and nebulous status of the Joseph tribes are thereby countered by a renewed presentation of a united Israel gathering within Ephraimite territory, and by the assertion that the land has been subjugated. The mention of the Tent of Meeting further confirms Israelite unity. Woudstra (1980:271), reading historically, suggests that setting up the Tent at Shiloh "was meant to counteract the tendencies toward disintegration which had shown themselves in the episode of the complaint of the Josephites." The concern for disintegration, however, is textual as well as historical. The assembly of Israel at the Tent of Meeting presents an image of concordance that reorients the story to a holistic and satisfactory conclusion.

Opposing this symbol of Yahweh's presence, however, are clear intimations of failure. Joshua's speech to the assembled tribes marks a return to an earlier means of achieving integrity. The allotment process is beginning again, but with a note of urgency:

> Joshua said to the Israelites, "How long will you be slack in entering to take possession of the land which Yahweh, the God of your ancestors, has given you?" (18:3)

The procrastinating tendencies of the Joseph tribes are now generalized to the rest of Israel. The entire congregation is upbraided for its lethargy in acquiring the land which Yahweh has given. To counter the inertia of the seven tribes (an intriguing number, in light of the number of nations said to be in the land; Deut 7:1), Joshua can do little more than return to an old procedure that has produced mixed results. He sends out a group of spies (three from each tribe, this time) and directs them to survey the land (18:4-8). Upon their return, the remaining territory is distributed by lot. Thus the final stage of the land's apportionment is initiated by a return to a more distant beginning, but in a context that conveys much less optimism than the previous occasion.

The tribal territory of Benjamin is the first to be elaborated (18:11-28). The description of its allotment, like that of Judah, is relatively detailed and gives the impression of completeness. The reader is presented with a clear delineation of boundaries, as well as a list of cities within the territory. This detailed definition serves the same purpose, at the outset of this section, as did that of Judah in the previous section. A complete depiction of tribal territory once more establishes a sense of integrity.

A closer examination, however, reveals a number of inconsistencies. Some of the cities listed in verses 21-24 seem to lie far north of the border shared with the Joseph tribes (cf. 16:1). In addition, some of the cities listed for Benjamin also appear in the list of cities assigned to Judah: Beth-Arabah (18:22; cf. 15:61) and Kiriath (18:27; = Kiriath Jearim [15:60?]).[12]

The territorial descriptions of the rest of the tribes (19:1-48) present even greater irregularity. Simeon and Dan, the second and seventh tribes, have no boundaries at all, while Issachar has only a fragmentary notice of a boundary line. These tribes live in territory that is ill-defined. When boundaries are delineated, moreover, as they are with the territories of Zebulun, Asher, and Naphtali, they are generally imprecise and incomplete. Likewise, although each of the tribal allotments contains a list of cities, it is clear from the territorial summaries that the reported cities comprise only a fraction of the cities actually located in each area: Zebulun reports twelve cities, although only five are listed; Asher reports twenty-two cities, with seven being listed; and so on. The report of the territories of the seven tribes thus follows the pattern of 15:1-17:18. In this pattern, the narrator presents a well-defined and homogenous territorial unit, but then continues with a series of other reports which depict tribal territories in a state of partial or complete disintegration.

The accounts of Simeon (19:1-9) and Dan (19:40-48) are especially noteworthy. In contrast to Benjamin, Simeon has no borders at all. And the cities listed for Simeon are also claimed by Judah, a fact which the narrator makes clear (19:9; cf. 15:26-32). Simeon thus represents an extreme case of tribal disintegration; the boundaries established to separate and define tribal integrity simply do not exist, leaving Judah and Simeon to mingle tribal territory and cities.

Dan's situation represents a different case of disintegration—the loss of allocated territory altogether.

> The territory of the Danites was lost to them, so the Danites went up and fought with Leshem. They captured it and struck it with the edge of the sword. They took possession of it and dwelt in it, and they renamed Leshem "Dan," after the name of Dan their ancestor. (19:47)

The Danites' story is deeply ironic. The narrator's explanatory comments mark the first actual account of a tribe's attempt to secure possession of its allotment. Yet the report communicates failure rather than success. The Danites are not able to establish themselves in the territory given to them, but travel to the extreme northern limit of the land. Their eventual possession lies outside the boundaries fixed for the other tribes and is but one city.

The description of Israel's lands in Canaan thus begins with the success of Judah and concludes with the failure of Dan. The entire corpus manifests the steady unraveling of coherence. One senses a degeneration from Caleb's victories and Judah's well-ordered territory to Dan's displacement and disintegration. The two accounts, moreover, are the only ones which actually relate how tribes took possession of their territories. What of the other tribes? The absence of such accounts further reinforces a sense of uncertainty. Did the other tribes fail to respond to the promise? Did they refuse to occupy the land assigned to them? Do the lists represent land actually possessed, or are they merely constructs, suggesting a potential (and promise) still awaiting fulfillment?

The apportionment to Joshua (19:49-50) concludes the distribution of land, just as the awarding of land to Caleb began it. The figures of Joshua and Caleb are not only connected by the structure of the text (their stories begin and end the description of tribal territories) but are also linked thematically (both had been faithful spies; Num 14:5-9).

Joshua, however, comes off poorly by comparison with Caleb. Both men are now old, but the vigorous Caleb asked for the hill country of Judah, a region inhabited by giants and guarded by large, fortified cities (14:12). Caleb's success and vigor corresponded to the comprehensive possessions of his tribe, Judah, whose tribal territory expresses a high degree of integrity.

On the other hand, Joshua asks for (and receives) a city in the hill country of Ephraim, which he builds himself. Joshua, the great hero of Israel, prefers the sparsely-settled hills over the giants of Canaan. The tribe he leads—Ephraim, the more dominant of the two Joseph tribes (Num 13:8)—follows suit, preferring to stay in the hill country rather than to go forth against fortified cities. And, in comparison to Judah, Ephraim's territory is filled with gaps and unfinished business.

The description of the land allocated to the tribes of Israel reveals a struggle between, on the one hand, desire for a structured portrait of life in the land, and, on the other hand, the presence of material that points toward dissolution. In a sense, the textual situation is like the geographical terrain it represents. It displays a general contour, with sections of integration and homogeneity, but the overall structure is severely fragmented.

LOOSE ENDS AND AFFIRMATION

The last phase in the organization of Israel's land concerns the cities of refuge and the Levitical cities (20:1-21:42). The report of the allocation of these cities marks another move to counter the now-disintegrated portrait of Israel. The designation of these cities was stipulated by Moses (Num 35:1-28), and their establishment at this point assumes the subjugation of the land. The narrator explicitly notes that the establishment of the required number of cities (six cities of refuge and forty-eight Levitical cities) was accomplished according to the directions of Moses (20:7-8; 21:41). By reporting the total implementation of the Mosaic directives, the narrative is once again brought under the sway of the ostensive plot, confirming that all the land has indeed been appropriated and apportioned.

Although the establishment of such cities represents integration and fulfillment, the groups that they shelter—manslayers and Levites—are themselves symbols of heterogeneity. The manslayers maintain a marginal status, perhaps in the service of the priesthood, until the guilt incurred by the taking of a human life is expiated by the death of the high priest (Greenberg 1959:125-32). The Levites, too, represent a marginal class of people. They do not receive an inheritance but are nonetheless given cities "to live in," along with surrounding pasturelands for their livestock (21:2-3).

Throughout the descriptions of tribal territories the reader is frequently reminded of the ambiguous status of the Levites. They are a tribe of Israel, and yet they are not counted as a tribe (13:14, 33; 14:2-4; 18:7). And just as notes about the Levites are interspersed throughout the text, so the Levites are interspersed throughout the territory of the tribes of Israel. Their presence among each of the tribes means that in each tribal area there is, by design, land not possessed by the tribe associated with that region. The issue is particularly thorny when it comes to the city of Hebron. Hebron is the city awarded to the zealous Caleb, yet it is also a city assigned to the Levites and designated as a city of refuge (21:11-13). Here the narrator has some explaining to do. The reader is told that the city itself is not given to Caleb, but to the Levites. Caleb receives the surrounding "fields and villages" (see, however, 14:14). But then who took Hebron, Joshua or Caleb? And to whom was it given, Caleb or the Levites?

Given the disordered and incomplete portrait of Israel rendered in the preceding accounts, the concluding summary is astonishing.

> Yahweh gave Israel all the land which he swore to give their ancestors. They took possession of it and lived in it. Yahweh gave them rest all around, according to all that he swore to their ancestors. Not one of their enemies stood before them. Yahweh put all their enemies into their hands. Not one promise failed, of every good promise which Yahweh made to the house of Israel. Every one was fulfilled. (21:43-45)

Such confident assertions are unexpected from the standpoint of what has been narrated previously. The gradual unraveling of territorial coherence is now emphatically blocked by an elaborate assertion of fulfillment: the land has been given, Israel has taken possession, Yahweh has given rest, and no one has been able to withstand Israel. This unequivocal pronouncement counters the sense of steady disintegration with an evaluation of Israel's story which asserts comprehensive possession of the land and affirms Israelite integrity. The desired ending is finally articulated, but the affirmations now seem hollow and surreal.

What is a reader to make of such abrupt and questionable assertions? As in other instances, interpreters of the book have often glossed the contradiction elicited by these claims. Many agree with the appraisal that they offer "a concise summary of the main theological affirmation of the book" (Miller & Tucker 1974:165). Others view the commentary as a description of an ideal never achieved (Kaufmann 1953:57-60). However, these readings deal inadequately with the glaring disjunction between narrated reality and narrative evaluation. The tension is too pronounced to be glossed, and the text gives little indication that the assertions are idealized.

The ironic sense of the text has been explored by both Polzin and Gunn. Polzin perceives irony on the ideological level of the text; the author/narrator, having led the reader to accept the point of view underlying 13:1-20:42, now presents a nonconcurrent point of view. The purpose of this procedure, according to Polzin, is to prompt a rejection of the "repeatedly exaggerated" claims made by the narrator (1980:127-32).

Gunn, on the other hand, senses irony "in the gap between the rhetoric of fulfillment and the rhetoric of completion" (1987a: 107-10). Fulfillment is what the commentary offers, but unfulfillment is what the reader has previously encountered.

In terms of the dynamic of plot traced previously, one may also understand 21:43-45 as a definitive reassertion of concordance and fulfillment. The abrupt juxtaposition of images of disintegration and unequivocal affirmation follows precisely the pattern repeated throughout the course of the book. The exaggerated claims represent an attempt to impose order on a story that has become increasingly incoherent and uncertain. Israel's integrity is compromised by fragmentary borders and the remnants of indigenous peoples in its midst. Yahweh, too, has yet to fulfill all he has promised—the Sidonians have yet to be dispossessed (13:6). By the time the tribal lands have been described, the story points to an incoherent and incomplete ending.

The decisive claims of 21:43-45, to which we now move, signal an escalation in the conflict of plots, laying bare the desire to master a now-intensified impulse toward fragmentation and incompletion. An extreme situation of disintegration is countered by an equally-extreme affirmation of fulfillment. The affirmation seems to offer an ending. After all, what more need be said if all the land has been taken and *every* promise fulfilled? Yet (and this is the irony) the words that *should* communicate satisfaction and a sense of closure instead elicit a profound sense of dissatisfaction. The tensions raised by Israel's failure to eliminate the peoples of the land are not resolved, and the fact that the story does not end here indicates that these threatening tensions cannot now be so easily repressed.

6

ENDINGS
AND
AMBIGUITY

A story's ending is conventionally the place where patterns are completed, connections between events clarified, and tensions resolved. A story that achieves a sense of closure does so by mastering resistances and reinforcing belief in an ordered reality in which everything has a meaning and explanation. However, as Joshua moves toward a conclusion, the tensions elicited by the story have intensified, not diminished. The story tries repeatedly to end, but cannot seem to do so.

"Endings" for Joshua are signaled by the affirmation of fulfillment in 21:43-45, by the return of the eastern tribes to the Transjordan (22:1-8), by the resolution of tension regarding the status of the eastern tribes (22:9-34), by the "farewell address" of Joshua (23:1-16), in the covenant ceremony at Shechem (24:1-28), and finally in the burials of Joshua, Eleazar, and the bones of Joseph (24:29-33).[1]

That the story continues after endings have been asserted reveals a series of unsuccessful attempts to gain mastery over the dissonances represented by Israel's disobedience and fragmentation. In the final segment of the book (Joshua 22-24), these dissonances are finally given explicit expression, and the contest of plots moves into the foreground. The threatened end—apostasy, expulsion, destruction—has been hinted at but not made explicit in the previous episodes. In each of the episodes comprising the final section (Joshua 22-24), however, this end is clearly articulated. The binding operation of desire is manifested as well, through the many indications, explicit and implicit, that the ending has been achieved. Joshua 22-24 thus reveals an intensification of the dynamic that has shaped the book from its beginning.

THE RIFT AT THE JORDAN

The return of Reuben, Gad, and half-Manasseh to the Transjordan signifies the completion of Israel's task in taking possession of the promised land. The report of their return (22:1-8) offers a strong promise of closure because, at the beginning of the book, these same tribes had confirmed their obligation to remain in Canaan until their kindred had achieved their "rest" (1:15-18; cf. Deut 3:20; Num 32:20-21). By reporting the return of the eastern tribes, the narrator therefore offers a confirmation of the evaluative assertions made in 21:43-45. The claim that Yahweh has given Israel "rest all around" (21:44) is reinforced by the report of an event that could only have taken place after that rest had been achieved (22:4).[2]

The report of the eastern tribes' return also manifests the desire to reassert and close the plots of integrity and obedience. Israel's achievement of the promised rest is explicitly affirmed in verse 4, and, as noted above, the very fact that Joshua releases the eastern tribes from their obligation reinforces the narrator's assertion that the task of possession has been successfully completed. Israel's fidelity is also strongly affirmed by a uniformly positive repetition of familiar signifiers of obedience. Joshua begins by giving effusive and unqualified praise to the eastern tribes.

> He said to them, "You have observed everything Moses the servant of Yahweh commanded you, and you have obeyed my voice in everything I commanded you. You did not abandon your kindred for the entire length of time until this day. You have observed the obligation to the commandment of Yahweh your God." (22:2-3)

The commendation is followed by a formal release from obligation (22:4). The proclamation of release consists of two parts, both of which are introduced by 'attah (commonly trans-lated "now"). The first is a declaration that the conditions for release have been met ("Yahweh your God has given rest to your kindred as he promised them"), and the second contains a repetitive directive to return to the Transjordan ("Return and go to your tents, to your landed property, which Moses the servant of Yahweh gave you on the other side of the Jordan").

Joshua concludes with an admonition which corresponds to that given him by Yahweh at the beginning of the book (22:5; cf. 1:7). The admonition is a virtual repetition of the charge to obedience which occurs frequently in Deuteronomy (cf. Deut 10:12-13, 20; 11:1; 6:4-15; 13:4-5; 30:15-20). Rendered in this way, Joshua's admonition thus conveys a sense that the story has come full circle.[3]

The narrator concludes appropriately by reporting that the eastern tribes did indeed return to their homes. The report is accompanied by two additional pieces of information. The first informs the reader twice that Joshua blessed the eastern tribes (22:6, 7b). The blessing is followed by a valediction in which Joshua enumerates the material blessings which the tribes now enjoy (vs. 8). According to Deuteronomy, Yahweh's blessing follows obedience (Deut 7:12-14; 15:4-5; 28:1-2; 30:15-16). The fact that the tribes receive and evidence blessing gives further confirmation of their fidelity to Yahweh and Moses.

Like the narrator's summary in 21:43-45, the report of the eastern tribes' return represents a forceful reestablishment of the ostensive plots through an overtly positive presentation of Israelite success, concordance, and obedience. The achievement of the desired ending is suggested by the repetition of positive signifiers (tsawah/"obey", shamar/"keep", and kol/"all" each occur six times within the first six verses, 22:1-6), and by explicit and implicit indications that the goal of "rest" and blessing has been attained. The report thus offers a likely and appropriate conclusion. The return of the eastern tribes appears to tie up the last "loose end" and affirms concordance and order.

The story fails to close, however, and continues on to relate the story of a conflict between the eastern tribes and the tribes in Canaan (22:9-34). The previous report has, in fact, anticipated this reopening. For one thing, Joshua's admonition to the eastern tribes suggests that fidelity to the law of Moses will become a controversial issue later. In addition, the narrator draws attention to the compromised integrity of Israel by breaking the frame of the narrative to remind the reader of Manasseh's broken condition (vs. 7). Manasseh's fractured state is, as the reader now knows, a microcosm of Israel's. Part of the tribe dwells in the land *Moses* gave, while the rest inhabits land assigned by *Joshua*.

The occasion for the conflict is the erection of an altar at the Jordan by the eastern tribes. The episode is but the latest manifestation of a long-standing tension within Israel's story, the root of which is the eastern tribes' insistence on dwelling on the other side of the Jordan.[4] The episode represents an avalanche of destructive images, forcefully articulating the dissonances which have threatened the sense of obedience and integration throughout the course of the book: apostasy, division, incompleteness, rebellion, divine wrath, defilement, and internecine warfare.

On the surface, the episode seems to concern an act of disobedience by the eastern tribes. The tribes in Canaan interpret the erection of the Jordan altar as an act of rebellion against Yahweh (22:16), presumably because it represents an alternative to the "altar of Yahweh our God" located at the site of the tabernacle (vs. 19). The existence of such an altar was expressly forbidden by Moses (Deut 12:1ff), and the Cisjordanian Israelites are clearly concerned that such flagrant disobedience will result in severe punishment for all Israel (vss. 17-21). The building of the altar is therefore denounced in the strongest terms, and the Israelites in Canaan prepare to take prompt and drastic action against their kindred in the Transjordan (vs. 12).

However, the structuralist analyses of Polzin (1980:134-41) and Jobling (1986:89-134) have shown that another concern is operative at a deeper level; namely a concern with the integrity of Israel. According to Polzin the narrative is really concerned with questions of definition. Whereas previous episodes have dealt with the problem of "outsiders" who had become "insiders," the present episode reverses the equation to deal with the question of "insiders" who have become "outsiders" by choosing to live outside the promised land. In Polzin's view, the central problem of the episode is the question of who belongs to Israel. The issue is brought to the fore by the narrative's emphasis on the separateness of the Transjordanians. Polzin discerns three techniques by which this separateness is indicated. First, an examination of how the Israelite tribes are named in the episode reveals that such terms as "the entire community" (22:12, 16, 18, 20) and "Israel/ites" (22:12, 22, 31, 32, 33) occur in contexts which assume the exclusion of the tribes of Reuben and Gad. Second, the fear voiced by the eastern tribes is particularly a fear that their descendants' inheritance in Israel will one day be disavowed (22:24-25). Finally, Polzin reminds the reader of the repeated use of 'br ("pass over/across") during the account of the Jordan crossing (3:1-4:15), an event that becomes a metaphor of Israel's passage from promise to fulfillment. The Israelite, he observes, is par excellence "the Hebrew" (ha'ibri). Because the "crossing over" has already taken place, the verb is not used in 22:9-34, except when the Cisjordanians exhort the eastern tribes to "cross over" and take a share in the land (22:19).

Jobling's reading of Joshua 22 is incorporated within a more extensive analysis that examines the larger story's perspective on the eastern tribes. Jobling notes that the Cisjordanian Israelites are concerned with the integrity of Israel and therefore perceive the Transjordanians' program as a disunification of Israel. Cisjordan Israel's program calls for geographical as well as ethnic unity. The Jordan is viewed as a boundary which effectively separates the eastern tribes from their kinspeople in the promised land, thus negating a sense of unity. The continued division of Israel is a dangerous and vexatious situation; dangerous because it may bring a negative response from Yahweh, and vexatious because the Transjordanians are needed to take up space currently occupied by Canaanites.

To build the altar is therefore to be disobedient as well as divisive. The episode threatens the two main lines of plot which configure the narrative. In previous instances, one of the two sets of plots is dominant; the issue is usually obedience or integrity. However, in the present instance, the two sets of plots coalesce. The altar symbolizes the dividing of Israel, and yet its construction is an act of disobedience which affects the entire people.

The episode begins harmlessly enough, with a second report that the eastern tribes returned to the Transjordan:

> The Reubenites, Gadites, and the half-tribe of Manasseh returned and departed from the Israelites at Shiloh, in the land of Canaan, in order to go to the land of Gilead, to their landed property, which they had obtained through the mouth of Yahweh by the hand of Moses. (22:9)

The open-ended wording of the report—they departed "in order to go"—intimates that something will happen on the way (Jobling 1986:103). Although formally an ending, the report actually looks ahead and marks the beginning of a new episode.

Before returning to their lands, the eastern tribes build an altar by the Jordan. It is clearly large enough to attract attention, being of "great appearance" (vs. 10b). Its location, however, is the source of some confusion. The narrator's description seems to place it on the west bank of the Jordan ("They went to the district of the Jordan, which is in the land of Canaan"; vs. 10a). Yet the Cisjordanian tribes appear to locate it on the east bank ("at the front of (*'el mul*) the land of Canaan, at the district of the Jordan, across from (*'el 'eber*) the Israelites"; vs. 11b). Boling (1982:512) remarks:

> [T]he reference could be to any point in the Jordan Valley, on either side of the river. Each succeeding phrase, ostensibly written to further pinpoint the area, only sustains the obscurity of the location.

Much of the tension in the story will derive from the perception of the Jordan as a boundary (vs. 25). As in other instances where the Jordan is so regarded (for example, Joshua 3-4), the reader encounters geographical ambiguity. A boundary is represented, but the narrator makes it difficult to orient oneself with reference to it.

The Cisjordanian tribes react swiftly, with a resolve and unanimity not evidenced since the early campaigns in Canaan. Once again, "the entire congregation of Israelites gathered at Shiloh" (22:12). The report is almost identical to the one which introduced the previous assembly at Shiloh (18:1a), leading the reader to contrast the two contexts and the Israel depicted in them. The connection with the previous assembly demonstrates how far Israel has disintegrated. In the previous instance, Joshua upbraided the tribes for their apathy and procrastination. Now that the tribes finally act decisively to make war, it is not against the Canaanites but against their own kindred. Joshua is conspicuous by his absence.[5] Furthermore, as Polzin has observed, "the entire congregation of Israel" is a name which now refers only to the western tribes.

Before initiating hostilities, the Cisjordanian tribes send a delegation to the eastern tribes in Gilead, presumably to see if the situation can be resolved through negotiation.[6] The central figure in the negotiations is Phinehas, the son of Eleazar. Why Phinehas rather than Joshua is chosen to lead the delegation we are not told, though a number of possibilities suggest themselves. Phinehas may be the protector of the Israelite cult, which has been threatened by a potential rival (Kloppenborg 1981: 354-55). Or Joshua's strong association with Ephraim may disqualify him as an impartial mediator in such delicate affairs. Then again, the presence of Phinehas is significant thematically. Phinehas was a central figure in the debacle at Peor (Num 25:1-18), where he played the role of executioner and avenger. His appearance in the present episode connects the two incidents, so that the specter of apostasy looms in the background. (The allusion to apostasy will become explicit as "the whole congregation" speaks.)[7]

The accusation against the eastern tribes is severe (22:16-20). It articulates the threatening, but so far submerged, tensions of the story. The opposing plots of disobedience and fragmentation now become explicit through caustic language, by explicit allusions to past disasters, by the subversion of positive symbols, and through the repetition of "day."

First, the delegation makes harsh and repeated allegations of disobedience. The building of the altar is portrayed in cataclysmic terms. The words of the delegation, who evidently speak for "the entire congregation" (vs. 16a) betray an astonishing intensity, as if the incident is a release of deeper hostilities. The eastern tribes have, throughout the book, been exemplars of obedience, but now they are excoriated with an exhaustive catalogue of recriminations: offense against God (*ma'al*; vss. 16, 20), apostasy (*shuv*; vss. 16, 18), rebellion (*mrd*; vss. 16, 18, 19), and iniquity (*'awon*; vss. 17, 20). These accusations accentuate the threat which the altar represents. *Ma'al* denotes a trespass on sancta or the violation of the covenant oath, offenses which inevitably invite divine retribution.[8] Adding to its seriousness, the term connects the present offense with Achan's crime. The term *'awon* makes a link with the incident at Peor and points up the residual defilement Israel has carried since its apostasy there (vs. 17). The common verb *shuv* ("turn"), often used of turning away from Yahweh, significantly recalls Moses' original warning to the eastern tribes:

> If you turn away from (Yahweh), he will again cause (Israel)
> to stay in the desert, and you will bring ruin on this entire
> people. (Num 32:15)

Finally, the root *mrd*, which occurs only twice in the previous narrative complex, recalls Israel's refusal to enter the land after the report of the spies (Num 14:9).

Second, although never specifying why the building of the altar is such a serious infraction, the delegation nevertheless places the act on a par with the most heinous and destructive sins of Israel's past. The allusions to Peor and Achan give the threatening aspects of this situation a dimension of terror. The altar, the delegation implies, is the first step toward idolatry (22:17), and its construction has somehow infringed on what rightfully belongs to Yahweh (vs. 20). In either case, all Israel is now at risk of infuriating Yahweh, who may at any time respond with plague (vs. 17) or an outpouring of wrath (vs. 20).

Third, the delegation's language overturns many positive symbols of obedience and integrity. No one had objected to the erection of the altar at Mount Ebal (8:30-35); on the contrary, it was constructed in obedience to the words of Moses and thus provided an occasion for Israel's integrity and fidelity to be affirmed. Now, however, the erection of the altar means the fracturing of Israel and threatens its destruction by Yahweh. The assembly of "the entire congregation," previously a marker of Israelite unity, now marks disunity and denotes only that part of Israel dwelling in Canaan. And when Israelite unity is mentioned, it is only in terms of its negative aspects—because of the action of a few, the entire people may endure Yahweh's wrath (22:20).

Finally, the repeated references to "today" and "this day" throughout the delegates' speech (five times within the speech; five more times throughout the chapter) convey a sense of urgency and immediacy. The many repetitions also remind the reader of the residue of other transgressions and fractures which remain, unresolved, to "this day" (6:25; 7:26; 9:27; 15:63; 16:10).

The charges against the eastern tribes are presented in two sections (vss. 16-18, 19b-20), each of which connects the building of the altar to a previous offense and its consequence. The repetition not only emphasizes the gravity of the indictment, but also draws attention to the short declaration lying between them.

> If, indeed, your landed property is unclean, then cross over to the landed property of Yahweh, where the tabernacle of Yahweh is located, and acquire (land) among us. (22:19a)

The declaration seems to have little to do with the virulent allegations made against the eastern tribes. Presumably, the delegation regards the east bank as unclean. Their declaration creates a dichotomy between the eastern and western tribes, bringing to the surface the repressed meaning of settlement in the Transjordan, which is that the integrity of Israel will be effectively and permanently broken. Nine and one-half tribes will live on the landed property of Yahweh, where Yahweh has chosen to place his dwelling. Two and one-half tribes will be separated from Yahweh (and the rest of Israel) in an unclean land.

Although the delegation has not said so, the eastern tribes interpret their allegations as really an expression of fear that the altar represents a rival cult. They respond to each of the harsh accusations leveled against them with equally emphatic denials.

> El, God, Yahweh! El, God, Yahweh! He knows! And let Israel know! If (it is) a rebellion (*mered*) or an offense against Yahweh (*ma'al*) do not save us this day. (If it is) to build an altar for ourselves to turn away (*shuv*) from Yahweh, or to offer burnt offerings or cereal offerings on it, or if to offer sacrifices of well-being on it, Yahweh will look into it. (22:22-23)

They then try to justify in detail the erection of the altar (vss. 24-29). They continue to protest that they did not intend to use the altar to offer sacrifices (vss. 24a, 26b, 28b), claiming instead that it has been constructed so that their descendants may not be separated from the rest of Israel. The delegation had insinuated that the eastern tribes were responsible for fracturing the integrity of Israel. Now the eastern tribes hurl the charge back at them, predicting that the descendants of the Cisjordanian tribes will be responsible for causing future division and apostasy in Israel.

> No! We did this out of concern for the situation, saying, "Tomorrow your children may say to our children, 'What have you to do with Yahweh the God of Israel? Yahweh has put a boundary—the Jordan—between us and you, you Reubenites and Gadites! You have no portion in Yahweh.'" So your children will make our children stop fearing Yahweh. (22:24-25; cf. 27b, 28a)

The altar, they retort, is not to function as an altar, but is actually a "copy" which will serve as a witness (*'ed*; a pun on *'edah*/"congregation"?) that the eastern tribes may continue to perform service to Yahweh. The explanation effectively overturns the symbol again, from apostasy back to fidelity. The altar, a "copy" of the one in Canaan, paradoxically becomes again a symbol of unity. Through this transformation, the conflict is resolved, and a catastrophic end is averted once more.

The eastern tribes' response ends as it began—with an oath, a denial of charges, and a disavowal of any intention ever to use the altar for the purpose of sacrifice (22:29). The entire explanation seems contrived and the denials are suspiciously passionate. The explanation itself borders on the implausible. (What is the purpose of an altar, if not to provide a place for sacrifice?) But Phinehas and the Cisjordanian chieftains are evidently interested in resolving the conflict and are therefore willing to accept the explanation at face value.

> Phinehas the priest, the chieftains of the congregation, and heads of the clans of Israel heard the words which the Reubenites, Gadites, and Manassites spoke, and it was good in their sight. (22:30)

The narrator's report reaffirms Israel's unity and once again puts to rest the story's dissonances. The threat of Yahweh's wrath also seems to be resolved. As Phinehas takes his leave of the eastern tribes, he confirms that "Yahweh is with us" and exonerates them of any offense against Yahweh (ma'al; vs. 31b). His verdict sanctions the tribes' explanation and affirms the restoration of Israel's relationship to Yahweh.

Phinehas' farewell indicates that these latest tensions have been resolved—except for his parting words to the eastern tribes:

> You have delivered the Israelites from the hand of Yahweh. (22:31c)

This is certainly a curious declaration! Phinehas speaks of the eastern tribes as saviors, while Yahweh is cast in the role of adversary. The language recalls the many times in which we have read that the peoples of the land have been given "into the hand" of Israel for destruction (2:24; 6:2; 8:1, 7; 10:8, 19, 30, 32; 11:8). Phinehas' last words remind the reader that Israel's habitation of the land remains tenuous.

The narrator nonetheless confirms that conflict is resolved by reporting that Israel as a whole agreed with the delegation's decision, acclaimed God, and talked no further of going to war to devastate the land of the eastern tribes (22:32). The episode concludes with the naming of the altar, designated "A Witness Between Us that Yahweh is God." The name asserts a closure of the ostensive plots: integrity ("A Witness Between Us") and obedience ("Yahweh is God"). Yet the altar has become an ambiguous symbol. Although confirming the integrity and obedience of Israel, it also stands as yet another reminder that Israel is fractured and liable to break its covenant with Yahweh.

JOSHUA'S FAREWELL

Joshua's address to assembled Israel (Josh 23:1-16) offers another occasion for a satisfactory ending. The chapter begins with a preface by the narrator, which once more affirms that Israel has attained the promised "rest" (23:1; cf. 22:4; 21:44) and reports that Joshua is "old and advanced in days." The statement of Joshua's age is virtually identical to that which opens the second section of the book (13:1). On the one hand, this temporal setting is a return to the beginning of the allotment process, with its summary of land not taken. Yet Joshua's advanced age suggests that he is near the end of his life, giving the reader the sense that his words may be perceived as a farewell address to Israel.[9] Similar addresses occur at key points in the larger narrative complex and signal the ending of major segments of Israel's history. Thus the reader might suspect that Joshua's speech brings the era of the land-acquisition to a close just as Deuteronomy functions as Moses' farewell address, and Samuel's speech in 1 Samuel 12 concludes the period of the Judges.[10] The context and content of the speech also suggest connections to the deathbed blessings of the Patriarchs (Genesis 48-40; 50:22-26) and the "last words of David" (2 Sam 23:1-7). Nearing the end of his life, Joshua is able to reflect on the end to which Israel has come. He speaks with the wisdom of one who is able to look back and discern the patterns and meaning of Israel's story.[11]

Joshua's "farewell" also corresponds to the initial addresses which began the book (1:1-18) and therefore serves as a narrative frame. Like the opening speeches, Joshua's final address is composed of phrases and themes drawn from Deuteronomy. In particular, Joshua confirms the promise that no one will withstand Israel (23:9b; 1:5a) and repeats the admonition to be strong and to observe carefully the entire *torah* of Moses, "turning neither to the right nor to the left" (23:6; 1:7). Furthermore, Joshua opens his speech with the words, "I am old and advanced in days" (23:2b), indicating that Yahweh's promise to be with Joshua "all the days of your life" (1:5) is nearing completion and fulfillment.

Joshua's speech also corresponds to Moses' address in Deut 4:1-40. In Deuteronomy, the account of the possession of the Transjordanian lands is followed by a reflective address, in which Moses recalls what Yahweh has done and exhorts Israel toward loyalty to Yahweh (Deut 4:1-40). Likewise, Joshua's address follows the narrator's information that the land has been possessed, and it exhibits similar content: repeated calls to obedience (Josh 23:6, 11; Deut 4:1-2, 6-9, 39-40), affirmations of Yahweh's part in dispossessing the inhabitants of Canaan (Josh 23:5, 9, 14; Deut 4:37-38), stern warnings against following the gods of Canaan (Josh 23:7, 12-13; Deut 4:15-20, 23-24), and a prediction that Israel will eventually be expelled from the land (Josh 23:15-16; Deut 4:25-28).

The farewell address of Joshua brings together the plots of obedience and integrity. However, as in the previous episode, certain dissonant strains are present—possession is incomplete and the temptation to turn to the gods of Canaan remains. These dissonances block a sense of fulfillment. In fact, Joshua's retrospective does not end by affirming the fulfillment of desire and expectation. Rather, his words aver the incompleteness of Israel's task and point to the possibility of an end outside the promised land.

The speech therefore represents a beginning, rather than the promised ending. More precisely, it signifies the *return* to a beginning. Joshua's words speak little of fulfillment, but place both Israel and the reader back in the realm of promise. The promises and admonitions uttered by Joshua echo those given to Israel in the period before it entered the land. The Israel now within the land is little different than the Israel which awaited entry into the land. Israel still waits for Yahweh to dispossess the inhabitants of Canaan (23:6), as it did in the time of Moses

(Exod 34:24; Num 32:21; Deut 4:38; 11:23). And Yahweh continues to demand obedience from Israel in the face of powerful temptations from the nations of Canaan and their gods (23:7, 12; cf. Exod 34:12-16; Deut 7:2-5; 12:29-31). The task of removing the inhabitants of the land remains, along with the warning that they will become the source of great trouble and irritation (23:12-13; Num 33:55-56).

The words of Joshua also emphasize the conditional nature of the promise and its fulfillment. True fulfillment has not yet been experienced, and will depend on Israel's uncompromising loyalty to Yahweh. Joshua emphasizes this point by predicting that Yahweh will dispossess the Canaanites (vss. 5, 9-10) and by strongly admonishing Israel to remain faithful (vss. 6-8, 11). The connection between Israel's obedience and the complete elimination of the Canaanites is made even more forcefully at the conclusion of the speech, when Joshua reasserts the claims of comprehensive fulfillment made at an earlier point by the narrator.

> I am going the way of all the earth. You know with all your heart and with all your soul that not one word—out of all the good words Yahweh your God spoke concerning you—has failed. Every one has been fulfilled for you. Not one of the words has failed. (23:14; cf. 21:45)

This is the same declaration, repeated with emphasis, that seemed incredible when given earlier! Yet now it is uttered by no less a figure than Joshua. There are, however, important modifications. First, the claims refer only to Yahweh; the assertions that Israel took possession of the entire land (21:43-44) are omitted. Second, whereas the claims made in 21:43-45 offered an unqualified assessment of success and fulfillment for Israel, the repetition of the promise is now joined by a prolepsis which intimates unfulfillment. The "good word" of Israel's past paradoxically points to the "evil word" of Israel's future (vs. 15) and thus foreshadows the exile which brings the larger story to an end.

> But just as every good word, which Yahweh your God spoke to you, has been fulfilled, so will Yahweh bring to pass every

evil word, until he exterminates you from this good land
which Yahweh your God has given you. (23:15)
The appended declarations transform the affirmation of the
promise into a threatening negation. The importance of this
transformation must not be underestimated. Joshua is not just
acknowledging the present reality of partial fulfillment. Rather,
he is pointing to a future in which the promise is forfeited
altogether. This counter-ending, which has been censored
throughout the course of the book, is clearly stated in his final
words.

When you transgress the covenant of Yahweh your God,
which he commanded you, and you go and serve other gods,
and bow down to them, then the wrath of Yahweh will burn
against you, and you will disappear quickly from the good
land which he gave to you. (23:16)

This conclusion has troubled many interpreters, who generally
have tried to soften the force of the opening phrase (*be'ov-
rekem*) by translating it as a conditional phrase ("If you transgress . . .").[12] While such a translation is possible, the context
argues against it, indicating that these comments predict Israel's
eventual expulsion from the land. As Butler (1983:253) puts it,
"the final and dominating word is a curse, and not a blessing."
What has been intimated throughout the book is now given
explicit expression. Israel will transgress the covenant, the wrath
of Yahweh will burn against Israel, and Israel will "disappear"
(*'avadtem*) from the land which it has been given. The occurrence of the verb *'avad*, which is often used to signify nomadic
existence or aimless wandering (cf. Lev 26:38; Deut 7:20; 8:19,
20; 11:17; 26:5; 28:20; 30:18), is especially noteworthy. The
prediction of Israel's disappearance looks ahead to a return to
landless existence (and so to disintegration). It thus blocks the
fulfillment of desire.

Joshua's farewell address to the assembled tribes would
seem a proper place to close the ostensive plots of the story, but
it overturns such expectations by making numerous references
to Israel's incomplete possession of the land and to the Israelites' potential to apostatize. The concluding remarks (vss. 15-16)

block any sense of resolution, presenting instead the undesired endings of disobedience and disintegration and expressing "a devastatingly negative expectation for the future of Israel in the land" (Boling 1982:256).

COVENANT RENEWAL AT SHECHEM

The book of Joshua concludes with the account of a covenant ceremony at Shechem (24:1-28), followed by a series of short reports (24:29-33). Like Joshua's address in 23:1-16, the episode at Shechem offers a reflection on Israel's past (24:2-13; 23:3-5), a challenge to the present (24:14-15; 23:6-13), and a preview of its future (24:19-22; 23:15-16). The same group gathers to hear this second speech (the elders, leaders, judges, and officers; 24:1; 23:1), and Joshua once again issues a series of stern admonitions forbidding the worship of other gods (24:2, 14-15, 19-20, 23; cf. 23:7, 12).

There are, however, significant differences. The reader is given a temporal reference for the assembly which gathers to hear Joshua's farewell (23:1b), but is not told where the gathering takes place (presumably Shiloh). Conversely, the reader is given an explicit geographical setting for the covenant ceremony in 24:1-28 (Shechem), but is given no sense of when the ceremony occurs. Furthermore, 24:1-28 deals with the worship of other gods as if it were a present reality, while 23:2b-16 seems to be regard apostasy as a potential which may yet be actualized by Israel's entanglements with the peoples of Canaan. Finally, while 23:1-16 consists of a monologue by Joshua, there are three speakers in 24:1-28: Joshua, Yahweh (through Joshua), and the people.

The covenant ceremony also raises certain questions. Does it present a significant contribution in its own right, or is it more in the nature of an appendix? Why is the ceremony related *after* Joshua's final address?[13]

The ceremony at Shechem is another attempt to assert a definitive ending. Joshua 23 concludes with an open-ended prediction that Israel will transgress the covenant, certainly not a definitive and satisfactory ending. The ceremony at Shechem in Joshua 24 counters that threatening prediction by showing that Israel confesses its fidelity to Yahweh and that it resolves to keep covenant. The passage elicits a sense of order and completeness. It exhibits a strong liturgical cast and is carefully structured to exhibit a symmetry of presentation.[14]

This is a well-formed narrative unit. References to "all Israel" (24:1, 27) and Shechem (24:1, 25) occur only at the beginning and end, providing frames for the passage. The content between these frames is also clearly organized. It opens with a historical review related by Yahweh through the mouth of Joshua (vss. 2-13), and introduced with the prophetic messenger formula ("thus says Yahweh"). An introductory *'attah* ("now"; vs. 14) signals a change from the review to an exhortation, which consists of a series of challenges by Joshua and affirmative responses by the people (vss. 14-24). The final section (vss. 25-28) is marked by a shift back to narrative and deals with the covenant at Shechem. The orderliness and directedness of this account is not to be overlooked, especially since it follows the rambling speech of Joshua in chapter 23. We now turn therefore to reading it in greater detail.

The episode begins by affirming the integrity and obedience of Israel; all the people of Israel gather at Shechem and present themselves before God (24:1). The reference to Shechem is somewhat surprising. The reader has been given no indication that the city was taken by the Israelites or that it bears any special importance to them (although the covenant renewal ceremony in 8:30-35 implies a gathering at or near Shechem). The setting is, however, significant. Beneath the oak at Shechem lie the idols of the "foreign gods" (*'elohey hannekar*) which the patriarch Jacob ordered his house to "put away" (Gen 35:1-4). It is therefore appropriate that the house of Jacob return there to put away the foreign gods in its midst and to confirm its fidelity to Yahweh (Josh 24:26).

The Jacob allusion signals a return to the beginning of Israel's story and confirms the fulfillment of the land promise first given to the patriarchs. The episode is therefore significant not only for the ending it provides the book of Joshua, but also for the sense of completion it offers the larger narrative complex. Whereas Joshua's farewell speech in 23:1-16 presented a reflection on the immediate past (all that Israel has seen Yahweh do to the nations of Canaan), the ceremony at Shechem situates Israel's experience within a broader context and pushes the story back to its patriarchal beginnings.[15]

The summary given in 24:2-13 is a recital of the stops along the way to fulfillment. It is the litany of a wayfaring people journeying to its promised place of rest. Composed of clipped phrases and action verbs, the entire recital exudes a dynamism that voices desire for an ending yet to be attained. In rapid sequence Yahweh chronicles Israel's odyssey, reminding Israel how it had been called into existence beyond the River in order to travel to, and enter, this new place.

The creation of this dynamism, moreover, is Yahweh's doing. The review is, in fact, a retrospective offered by Yahweh, as the opening messenger formula makes clear. It is stacked with first person verbal forms—"I took," "I gave," "I brought," etc.—which accentuate Yahweh's dynamic role in Israel's story. Yahweh has made things happen for Israel, intervening time and again to move events forward toward an acceptable end. Israel, in contrast, has been a passive participant in its own story—more object than subject. This is no more apparent than in Yahweh's final words to Israel.

> I gave you a land on which you did not toil and cities which you did not build. And you settled in them, eating from vineyards and olive trees which you did not plant. (24:13)

This prophetic retrospective powerfully asserts that the fulfillment of Yahweh's promises is almost entirely due to the many deeds Yahweh has done on Israel's behalf.[16] Yahweh has been faithful to give Abraham many descendants (24:3) and to bring Israel into the land of Canaan. Yahweh has given guidance and protection to Israel and has dispossessed the inhabitants of the land. As the review emphasizes Yahweh's graciousness action and Israel's passive reception, the distinct impression is given that Yahweh is the central figure in Israel's story; perhaps more so than Israel itself.

Yahweh's historical review (via Joshua) asserts that every expectation aroused by the promises to Israel's ancestors (cf.

23:14; 21:45) has been fulfilled. Yet the fulfillment of the promise depends as much on Israel's response as it does on any
activity by Yahweh. The chain of indicatives thus gives way to
a sequence of imperatives as Joshua exhorts his listeners to fear
and serve Yahweh and to put away all other gods. In this way
Joshua links the end to the beginning and challenges Israel to
complete the narrative by putting away the gods which still tie
it to its beginnings "beyond the River" and "in Egypt" (24:14).

Joshua's challenge offers an explicit opportunity for the
plots of integrity and obedience to reach a satisfactory conclusion. Israel is called to serve Yahweh "completely and with
fidelity." Israel's response to Yahweh must be total and unas-
sailable. To stress the point, Joshua repeats the verb 'avad ("to
serve") seven times as he presses Israel to make a choice either
for Yahweh or for the gods of the nations (vss. 14-15).

The assembly's response is gratifying. In language recalling
the eastern tribes' earlier protestation, the people begin with a
negative: "Far be it from us to abandon Yahweh to serve other
gods" (vs. 16). Likewise they end with a clear confession of
allegiance: "We will indeed serve Yahweh, because he is our
God" (vs. 18b). In the process, they also affirm the review of
their story offered earlier, declaring that Yahweh "protected us
everywhere we went and among all the peoples through whom
we traveled" (vs. 17b). Their concluding declaration of intention
to serve Yahweh is clear and unequivocal.

Joshua's response to Israel's confession is startling:

> Then Joshua said to the people, "You will not be able to
> serve Yahweh, because he is a holy God. He is a jealous God.
> He will not forgive your rebellion or your sins. If you abandon
> Yahweh and serve foreign gods, he will turn and bring calami-
> ty on you. And he will make an end to you after the good he
> has done for you." (24:19-20)

At no other point has the appearance of dissonance been so
surprising—or so unwelcome. Just at the point of affirmation
and closure, Joshua disputes the people's declarations with a
denial of their ability to honor their commitment. As in the
previous chapter, the words of Joshua become a medium for

articulating the opposing plots, and once again the endings these plots point to are made explicit.

Joshua's rejection of the people's confession is all the more striking given his role in the larger story. Joshua is the mediator of the covenant and therefore stands between Yahweh and Israel. In this capacity, his function is to bring the two parties together and effect a union between them. Both parties are willing to enter into the covenant relationship. Yet, ironically, it is precisely the covenant mediator standing between the two who seems to be keeping them apart! Yahweh will not unite with Israel, Joshua says, because he is a holy and jealous God who refuses to forgive Israel's sin. Israel cannot unite with Yahweh, Joshua further states, because Israel is unable to remain faithful and desires other gods.

The reference to foreign gods is somewhat unexpected. They have not appeared before in the book, but Joshua speaks of them as if they have been present among the people for some time. These "foreign gods" are specifically the gods of Canaan (Gen 35:2, 4; Deut 31:16; Jer 5:19). Joshua's words powerfully recall an earlier repressed prediction, uttered at the end of another story:

> Yahweh said to Moses, "You are going to rest with your ancestors. But this people will arise and prostitute themselves after the foreign gods of that land which they are entering. They will abandon me and invalidate my covenant, which I made with them. My anger will burn against them on that day, and I will abandon them and hide my face from them. They will be consumed, and many calamities and afflictions will find them. And they will say on that day, 'Is it not because Yahweh is not among us that all these calamities have found us?' But I will surely turn my face away on that day because of every evil thing they have done, because they turned to other gods." (Deut 31:16-18)

This prophecy to Moses, speaking of foreign gods and a broken covenant, clearly resonates in Joshua's prediction, and opposes the people's attempt to bring fulfillment through confession of allegiance to Yahweh. The reader is left to ponder how these foreign gods could have made their way into the congregation of Israel. The answer, however, is not difficult to discern. Israel has made other covenants with the people of Canaan, sparing them and bringing them into its corporate existence (6:25; 9:27). Vast enclaves of Canaanites also remain amidst the territories allotted to Israel's tribes. Moses's words, recently echoed by Joshua, make the consequences of such a situation very clear. If any of the erstwhile inhabitants of the land are allowed to survive, they will lead Israel away from Yahweh to serve other gods (Deut 7:1-6).

The threat of apostasy and destruction is then countered by the people's repeated affirmation that they will indeed serve Yahweh (24:21). But Joshua interprets their declaration ambiguously and thus weakens its force:

> You are witnesses against yourselves that you have chosen to serve Yahweh. (24:22)

To be "a witness against" ('*ed b*-) often refers to an indictment (Num 5:13; Deut 19:16; Prov 24:28; Mic 1:2). Joshua's response therefore seems another challenge to the people's pledge.

The people, however, are not easily put off. They quickly confirm Joshua's words, prompting Joshua to issue yet another admonition to "put away the foreign gods among you and turn your hearts to Yahweh the God of Israel" (24:23). However, it is the people who bring the dialogue to a close with an emphatic repetition of their intention to serve and obey Yahweh (vs. 24).

The dialogue between Joshua and the people reveals the contest of plots, now intensified as the narrative nears its conclusion. In this contest, the people articulate the plots of obedience and integrity, voicing a unanimous and unequivocal resolve to serve Yahweh. The declaration "we will serve Yahweh" is asserted three times in the course of the dialogue (vss. 14-24), expressing the strength of the desire to end the story with the expected depiction of a unified and obedient Israel. The opposing plots of disobedience and fragmentation appear unexpectedly (as they have throughout the narrative) in the words of Joshua. These plots present a contrary ending, in which Israel is disobedient and Yahweh "makes an end" to both people and promise.

The contest seems to be resolved in favor of the ostensive plots (obedience and integrity). The people have the last word. Their affirmations are confirmed by the report that Joshua made a covenant for the people, recorded its stipulations and terms in the *torah of God,* and erected a monument under the oak at the sanctuary of Yahweh (24:25-26). Each of these three actions gives a strong symbolic reinforcement to the sense that the story is closing on a positive and satisfying note. The covenant ceremony has functioned previously to signify Israel's obedience (cf. 8:30-35, at the same location?), as has the reference to *torah* (1:7-8; 8:30-35). And the oak at Shechem is, as noted above, a holy place of particular significance.

Yet this covenant ceremony also resonates ominously, for the covenant is made against portents of apostasy and curses. Even as it is made, the reader anticipates its transgression and the visitation of divine wrath. Perhaps it is broken even as it is ratified.

The great stone at the sanctuary is a particularly ambiguous symbol, for Joshua declares that it will be "a witness against us" (a declaration which is repeated for emphasis; 24:27). It appears that the last word will belong to Joshua after all. The pronouncement not only brings a proleptic charge against the people, but also connects the stone, and what it symbolizes, directly to the altar built by the eastern tribes. The altar at the Jordan is also a witness, ostensibly of the unity and obedience of Israel (22:34), but at a deeper level of the division and threatened apostasy represented by Reuben and Gad. The stone under the oak displays a corresponding ambiguity, marking Israel's devotion to and rejection of its God.

THE END OF THE STORY

The notice that Joshua dismissed the people is followed by a short appendix consisting of a series of burial reports (24:29-33). The reports of the deaths and burials of Joshua and Eleazar render a sense of finality to the story of Israel's entry into the land, while the report of Joseph's bones being buried at Shechem signals the closure of the larger story.

Yet even here there is uncertainty. A final remark is offered by the narrator after the report of Joshua's burial.

> Israel served Yahweh all the days of Joshua and all the days of the elders who outlived Joshua, and who knew every deed Yahweh had performed on behalf of Israel. (24:31)

With this comment, the narrator seems to align with the people ("we will serve Yahweh"; vss. 18b, 21, 24) against Joshua ("you cannot serve Yahweh"; vs. 19) and thereby asserts an ending which satisfies narrative desire. Yet, as with previous evaluations, the narrator's assertion does not entirely put to rest the story's considerable tension. If making oaths and covenants with the peoples of the land is consistent with serving Yahweh, then the narrator's evaluation of events is trustworthy. The reader knows, however, that these oaths and covenants violate the commandments of Yahweh. Why is there no report that the congregation ever put away the foreign gods, as Joshua challenged them to do? An ending is presented, but the story remains in suspension.

The conclusion of the book of Joshua is brought about by the death of Joshua and ostensibly affirms the fulfillment of desire; an obedient Israel is now settled in the land. It completes expectations elicited at the beginning, offering coherence and satisfying the desire for fulfillment. But it is also superficial and ambiguous. The narrator's affirmations do not adequately address and dissipate the powerful tensions maintained throughout the story. Israel acts as a unit to the very end, but it is also divided and incomplete. Israel has seen Yahweh bring victory after victory against overwhelming odds. Yet its land is pockmarked by enclaves of Amorites who tempt it to serve other gods. Israel affirms its intention to serve Yahweh, but shows a disturbing tendency to disregard Yahweh's statutes and lives under the dark cloud of predicted apostasy.

The closure of the ostensive plots is therefore not entirely successful in bringing about the sense of an ending. The many instances of transgression, division, and apathy, as well as the predictions of Joshua and Moses, indicate that the ending yet resides in the future. And it does not promise to be a pleasant one.

The book concludes by presenting an ending that articulates closure and resolves tension. Yet the emphatic finality of the burial reports is at variance with the repeated episodes of Israelite disobedience and failure. The gap between fulfillment and unfulfillment issues a challenge to the reader and exposes the desire for coherence and satisfaction. How far is the reader willing to go to achieve the sense of fulfillment that he or she expects? To what extent is the reader willing to collaborate with the text in repressing and glossing the dissonances that threaten chaotic and undesired endings? What is gained and lost by affirming the ostensive plots of the book against those which disrupt?

7

CONCLUSION

ISRAEL'S DESIRE

Within the context of the story, Israel's desire is clearly for the land. Canaan is "a land flowing with milk and honey" (Num 14:8; Deut 11:9), offering rest, security, and abundance. Life in the land represents "the goal and desire of the people of God" (P. D. Miller 1969:453). Yet more than a destination, it promises a profound fulfillment—Israel in the land is Israel identified, coherent, and completed.

Life in the land is also life with Yahweh, who gives the land (Josh 1:2-5; 13:6-7)[1] and confirms the promise by removing those who stand as obstacles to Israel's fulfillment (Josh 8:18; 10:11; 11:6; 23:5, 9-10).[2] Yet Yahweh also represents the dominant threat to Israel's satisfaction. The peoples of the land constitute no real peril for Israel as long as Yahweh is with them. However, Israel is doomed to failure if Yahweh withdraws (Josh 7:1-12). Even worse, Israel clearly fears that Yahweh may change from helper to adversary and inflict on them the fate visited upon the people of Canaan. Israel therefore strives to observe the commandments given by Moses so that it may enjoy life in the land. From Israel's perspective, obedience to the commandments is important not only to ensure Yahweh's aid but also to avoid his wrath.

YAHWEH'S DESIRE

Yahweh's desire follows a different trajectory. Although Yahweh speaks infrequently, his desire has been articulated through the

141

words of Moses. Yahweh's desire is for Israel—specifically for communion with Israel as signified by the covenant. The language Yahweh uses when speaking of Israel is often the language of desire; Israel is chosen (*bahar*; Deut 4:37; 7:6, 7; 10:15; 14:2), loved (*'ahav*; Deut 7:8, 13; 23:6), desired (*hashaq*; Deut 7:7), and treasured (*segullah*; Deut 7:6; 14:2; 26:18).[3] Similar language is also employed when Yahweh describes the response he wishes from Israel (Deut 6:5; 10:12; 11:13; 19:9; 30:6). Yahweh's desire for Israel will be satisfied, in other words, when Israel responds in kind.

What, then, threatens Yahweh's desire? Ironically, the answer would seem to be the land—Yahweh's gracious gift to Israel. The land threatens, both directly and indirectly, to draw Israel away from Yahweh. The direct threat issues from the gods of Canaan, who appear as rivals for Israel's allegiance. Indirectly, the abundance of the land tempts Israel to turn away. When its needs are satisfied by the land, Israel may no longer need or desire Yahweh, making other gods all the more tempting (Deut 8:10-20). Israel's satisfaction may thus come at the expense of Yahweh's.

The land is a threat because of Israel's inconstancy. Yahweh is clearly anxious that the people he has chosen will choose other gods, and expresses this concern repeatedly even before Israel enters the land.[4] The commandments given to Israel therefore express Yahweh's desire for Israel's fidelity. This is especially apparent when one considers the explanations given for the severity of the laws concerning the people of Canaan. Israel is admonished to destroy the peoples of Canaan because they present a danger to Israel's relationship with Yahweh; if the people of Canaan are allowed to remain in the land, they will ensnare Israel with their gods (Num 33:55-56; Deut 7:4; 12:29-31; 20:17-18).

It is by no means insignificant that when Moses warns of a disastrous end for Israel—extermination or expulsion from the land—the predicted end is almost always explained as the result of Israel's abandonment of Yahweh for other gods.

> All the nations will say, "Why has Yahweh done this to this land? What is this fierce, smoldering anger?"

142

> They will say, "Because they abandoned the covenant which Yahweh, the God of their ancestors, made with them when he brought them out of the land of Egypt. They went and served other gods, and worshiped them—gods whom they did not know and he did not assign to them. Yahweh's anger burned against this land, so that he brought upon it all the curses written in this book. Yahweh uprooted them from their land in anger, wrath, and fury, and he sent them to another land, as it is to this day." (Deut 29:23-27)

The wrath which Israel fears comes when the desired relationship with Yahweh is broken in Israel's pursuit of other relationships (Exod 23:24; Deut 6:13-15; 8:18-19; 11:28).

The desires of Israel and Yahweh are therefore oriented in different directions as the book of Joshua unfolds. Yahweh and Israel want different things. Yet both seek an end that is not fulfilled. Israel desires fulfillment and security in the land. It enters the land knowing of Yahweh's promise to dispossess its inhabitants and enjoys many victories. But no sooner does it enter the land than it begins to succumb to its temptations. Israel is not above bending the rules a bit if doing so makes things easier, and once in the land, it is all too happy to settle for what it has already acquired rather than finish the task. There is a desire for obedience on Israel's part, but it is somewhat equivocal. Israel does not quite understand what underlies the commandments it receives.

Yahweh's desire is for Israel, specifically for its allegiance. This desire is articulated throughout the narrative and is apparent in Yahweh's forbearance; even though Israel breaks the prohibitions against agreements with the nations, Yahweh nevertheless continues to aid Israel. Yet Yahweh can be provoked by Israel's response to the allure of Canaan. And when thus provoked, he demands a punishment reserved for those who entice Israel to follow other gods (Josh 7:13-15; cf. Deut 13:1ff). This is the predicament of Yahweh which the final speech of Joshua at Shechem reiterates. Even though Yahweh has been faithful to Israel, Israel continues holding to other gods. Joshua's final words to Israel are therefore invested with climactic significance, and the concluding debate brings to the surface the book's many ambiguities. Will Israel find a relationship with Yahweh ultimately desirable? Will the people put away the foreign gods to serve Yahweh, or will they serve the foreign gods and thus experience disaster at the hands of Yahweh? Does Israel even have the capacity for fidelity?

THE NARRATOR'S DESIRE

The narration of the story itself indicates an undercurrent of struggle and ambiguity. The narrator's desire seems to be oriented toward an ending which affirms an obedient Israel dwelling without rival in the promised land. This desire is manifested in the presentation of episodes, such as the Jordan crossing or the erection of the altar on Mount Ebal, which accentuate Israel's obedience and integrity. It is also manifested by a consistently positive (and at points hyperbolic) interpretation of events.

Yet the narrator also presents instances of Israel's disobedience, failure, and fragmentation, often immediately after affirmations of success or obedience. The stories of Rahab, Achan, and the Gibeonites, for example, counter affirmations of Israel's fidelity or Yahweh's gracious response to Israel. Likewise, affirmations of comprehensive victory are countered by troublesome exceptions, and well-ordered descriptions of boundaries are opposed by fragmenting reports of land not taken.

The patterning of obedience and integrity represents, fundamentally, a desire to assert order and coherence. The covenant and the land serve as the metaphors by which Israel is defined. These metaphors must remain intact so that Israel's identity can be established. The fidelity and integrity of Israel, and its complete possession of the land, are therefore vigorously asserted.

The maintenance of these metaphors becomes increasingly difficult as the story develops. The concordance between Israel and Yahweh, signified by the covenant, is repeatedly disrupted by the development of rival relationships. Israel's identification with the land is compromised by large areas still inhabited by indigenous peoples. And Israel's story cannot be told apart from the stories of other peoples, who remain with Israel "to this day."

THE READER'S DESIRE

The operation of plots in Joshua prompts a reflection on one's own investment in coherent representations of reality. An ostensible framework is offered, incoherences are repeatedly countered, and an affirmative ending is presented. Yet the story is untidy and resistant. The operation of plot in Joshua, in a sense, mirrors the difficulty of applying dogma to the experience of life. Our structuring operations are essential. We cannot effectively engage the world without them. Yet experience often seems to exceed our constructs. Reality resists and provokes our concords with dissonances and uncertainties. Israel laid claim to fulfillment, but continued to tell its story under the impulse of a promise yet to be realized.

NOTES

BIBLIOGRAPHY

INDEXES

NOTES

NOTES TO CHAPTER 1:
INTRODUCTION

1. There is considerable debate regarding the number and character of the deuteronomistic editions of the book. The major positions have been presented in the seminal work of Martin Noth (1967), who asserts one deuteronomistic editor, and Rudolph Smend (1971), who finds evidence for a series of deuteronomistic redactions. There are also questions concerning the provenance of the materials in Joshua 13-21 and the point of their inclusion within the framework of the book. For a detailed survey of the various positions on these and other issues of composition, see Auld (1980).

2. Brevard Childs points to the importance of recognizing that the editors of the book chose to preserve the tensions (1979:247-53).

3. Both Gunn (1987a) and Eslinger (1989) explore the dimensions of irony presented by the tensions in the text.

4. Elizabeth Dipple (1970) offers an excellent summary of the development of ideas of plot from Aristotle to the 20th Century.

5. Westermann uses his scheme to identify the pristine narrative material of the various units, noting whether or not particular materials conform to the tensive arc. Any material that does not conform to this singular pattern is deemed extraneous.

6. For a fuller discussion, see Chatman (1978:42-63), Rimmon-Kenan (1983:6-23), and Genette (1980).

7. Sternberg asserts that while the latter type of transformation is secondary in Aristotle's system, it is the primary mode of plot in biblical narrative, expressing an ideology that opposes divine omniscience to human ignorance (1985:172-85).

8. Structuralism in particular has been criticized for reducing plot to a system of logical sequences, a procedure which, it is argued, fails to address the temporality, dynamism, and complexity of literary plots. The criticism of Paul Ricoeur (1980:178) is representative:

> Structuralists . . . take it for granted that the surface grammar of what they call the "plane of manifestation" is episodic and therefore purely chronological . . . . They do not see that the

humblest narrative is always more than a chronological series of events and that in turn the configurational dimension cannot overcome the episodic dimension without suppressing the narrative structure itself.

9. An excellent summary of current literary approaches is provided by Terry Eagleton (1983).

NOTES TO CHAPTER 2:
ELEMENTS OF THE PLOT

1. The Exodus account is more overtly theophanic than Joshua's encounter. Soggin (1972:76-78) asserts, with little evidence, that the commander of the army of Yahweh functions as a hypostasis of Yahweh here.

2. I am translating the third masculine singular suffixes in this context as plurals.

3. A particularly fine discussion of narrativity is offered by Kort (1988:6-23).

4. Roy Shafer (1980) maintains that the impulse to order human experience is essential to the integration of human personality and subjectivity, noting that psychic disintegration often accompanies the disintegration of one's personal narrative.

5. Paul Ricoeur discusses the concord-making activity of narrative at length in the first volume of *Time and Narrative* (1984).

6. The adoption of this paradigm has been widespread, although there are numerous refinements in terminology. A useful overview of the general discussion, along with an analysis of the relationship of story to plot, is given by Egan (1978).

7. Ricoeur, however, prefers to speak of the distinction in terms of "event" and "story".

8. The reader's role in filling textual gaps, or "blanks," with his or her own projections has been explored thoroughly by Wolfgang Iser (1978). Chatman (1978:43-53) gives a particularly useful discussion concerning conventions of plot and the way these conventions are "naturalized" by the reader.

9. Bar-Efrat (1989:93ff) discerns three principal relationships at work in the connections which biblical narrative forges between events: cause and effect, parallelism, and contrast.

10. Both Sternberg (1985:365-440) and Alter (1983) extensively discuss forms of repetition. Sternberg catalogues formal repetitions and analyzes their use in the biblical text.

11. See further Kermode 1966.

12. These notions of verisimilitude, however, are conventional. See Chatman (1978:48-53).

13. See further Brooks (1984:90-112).

14. Brooks cites the work of French semiotician Émile Benveniste to support his argument at this point. See further Brooks (1987:11-12).

15. The collusion between text and reader is ably demonstrated by Elizabeth Wright (1987:90-103), who offers a study of texts which evoke a response before the reader has the opportunity for interpretation. Such texts illustrate the reader's impulse to project unconscious desires. Also see Brooks (1987:14-15).

NOTES TO CHAPTER 3:
CONQUEST AND COMPROMISE

1. See Thompson (1976:65-66).

2. Regarding the lax application of the ban in Joshua 1-12, D. J. McCarthy remarks, "We may note that the only acceptable way to avoid the ban is to make a covenant with Israel" (1971:174).

3. See Polzin (1980:16-24,84-91,117-127).

4. Butler hints at this and views the hardening of the Canaanites' hearts as Yahweh's attempt to make "Israelite obedience easier" and "to protect Israel from the major sin of idolatry" (1983:130).

5. This issue is explored in a provocative reading by Eslinger (1989:25-54), who suggests that it is something of an embarrassment. Yahweh had promised to harden the hearts of the Canaanites and drive them out but does not seem to be doing his part in Joshua. The answer to this puzzle, Eslinger suggests, is given later in Judges.

6. See Gunn (1987a:120).

7. For a fuller discussion of the significance of the land, see Brueggemann (1977).

8. For a more complete discussion of the connection of the land with a sense of identity, see Peter Diepold, who remarks that being in the land is constitutive for Israel's sense of being (1972:143).

9. The transformation of the land promise from indicative to imperative is addressed from a compositional perspective by von Rad (1966:79-93) and Diepold (1972:86-88).

10. The term occurs approximately 120 times in Joshua.

NOTES TO CHAPTER 4:
OBEDIENCE AND DISOBEDIENCE

1. Christoph Barth (1971:44-56) argues that Israel's response displays a form which he calls the "Answer of Israel" and cites many

other examples from the Hebrew Bible in which this form has been preserved. The structure of the response represents the dialogue of Israel as a part of an Israelite cultic liturgy, and expresses Israel's readiness to follow Yahweh's stipulations. However, in Josh 1:10-18 the answer is not given by all Israel, but by the eastern tribes. If the text did exist in such a form before inclusion, the form seems to have been appropriated in an ironic fashion.

2. See Ginzberg (1909:4-6).

3. For this view, see Miller & Tucker (1974:30). Siegfried Wagner (1964:255-269) posits a preexistent "spy report" form, which he links to the holy war tradition.

4. The connection has been widely acknowledged; see Miller & Tucker (1974:31).

5. For more on the prostitute as threat, see Bird (1989:119-140). She describes the prostitute as "a predator, preying on the weakness of men, a mercenary out for her own gain, an opportunist with no loyalty beyond herself, acknowledging no principle or charity in her actions" (130).

6. The verb *shakav* ("lie") is not synonymous with *lun/lin* ("to lodge"), as is suggested by many translations. Those occurrences which may be advanced to assert such a parallel (Lev 14:47; 2 Kgs 4:11; 9:16) are highly ambivalent.

7. For a discussion of *zonah* ("prostitute") as it is used in this context, see Boling (1982:145), Gray (1967:64), and Soggin (1972:39-41).

8. Woudstra (1980:69-70), for example, agrees that the house of Rahab is a brothel but seeks to justify the presence of the spies by arguing that this location was chosen because it would enable the spies to gather information while escaping detection.

9. The verbs which signify Rahab's actions in hiding the spies are to be regarded as pluperfects; see McCarthy (1971:170-71).

10. The characterizations of Rahab and the spies indicate a reversal of conventional gender roles.

11. McCarthy (1971a:173-74) interprets the passivity of the spies as "an excellent example of man's part in holy war" (cf. also 1971b:228). Their passivity allows Yahweh to orchestrate the entire series of events.

12. Langlamet (1971:180-83), in the course of a compositional analysis, detects a high correspondence in vocabulary with Genesis 19 and Genesis 24. From this, he argues that Joshua 2, like the Genesis texts, are to be attributed to the Yahwist tradition. He apparently does not, however, notice the connection between the two stories.

The similarities between the two stores (Genesis 19 and Joshua 2) suggest that a type-scene convention is being utilized in an ironic fashion. For more information on the type-scene, see Alter (1981).

13. This term also conveys sexual overtones.

14. The deuteronomistic character of this confession is widely acknowledged and is usually regarded as an expansion by a deuteronomistic editor, who has inserted it to emphasize the unique authority of Yahweh; see Butler (1983:33).

15. K. M. Campbell (1972:243-44) detects elements of a covenant-form in Rahab's speech: Preamble (2:11b), Prologue (vss. 9-11a), Stipulations (vss. 12-13), Sanctions (vss. 18-20), Oath (vss. 14, 17), and Sign (vss. 18-21).

16. Tucker (1972:66-86) notes that the narrator's report of the spies' escape stands between the spies' acceptance of the oath and the conditions they put on the oath and regards the uneven style here (and elsewhere) as indicating the passage's complex prehistory.

17. Translators generally treat the first two sentences, *naqim 'anahnu mishshevu'atek hazzeh 'asher hishba'tanu* and *hinneh 'anahnu ba'im ba'arets*, as dependent clauses, connecting the phrases of 2:17b-21a together. From this perspective, the spies' words mean something like "we will be innocent if . . . when we come into the land, you tie the cord, gather your family." This translation may derive from a preconception that the spies must be acting in fidelity to the oath with Rahab, rather than trying to back out of it. However, the grammatical form of the phrases indicates that these are to be regarded as independent clauses, a reading confirmed by the Septuagint translation. Both sentences have as their subjects the independent pronoun *'anahnu* ("we"). The first is a nominal sentence in which the spies protest their innocence. There is no indication in the text that it should be regarded as a conditional clause. Likewise, the second (introduced by *hinneh/* "behold") is a statement confirming that Israel is indeed about to enter Canaan (a statement made only now, when the spies are almost free and clear). The statement stands on its own, separated from the previous sentence by *hinneh* and from the following sentence by the latter's placing of the direct object as the first component of the sentence (*'et-tiqwat hut hashshani hazzeh*). The compound sentence which follows (vss. 18b-19) gives directions and spells out the conditions of the oath on Rahab's end. Grammatically, however, a conditional clause cannot be found until the *we'im-taggidi* which begins verse 20. See my translation above in the main body of text.

18. This was an interpretation given by early Christian interpreters; see Gray (1967:66), Soggin (1972:42), Woudstra (1980:75).

19. See Bird (1989:130).

20. The Groom describes the Bride's lips with the same metaphor: "like a thread of scarlet (hut shani) are your lips" (Cant 4:3a), a provocative image given the sexual overtones in the episode.

21. The liturgical aspects of the narrative have been elaborated by Jay Wilcoxen (1968:43-70), who makes a case for regarding chapters 1-6 as a unit linked together by liturgical concerns. See also Polzin's discussion (1980:92-94).

22. A detailed analysis of the promise/fulfillment scheme of the Jordan crossing is offered by Polzin (1980:104-110) and Saydon (1950:194-207).

23. Polzin (1980:107-110) discusses at length the relationship between the Ark and the obedience of Israel. However, he regards the stability of the Ark in the midst of the Jordan as a signifier of the exact fulfillment of the word of the Lord, while the setting up of stones in the Jordan refers to the possibility of interpreting the Mosaic law.

24. Christopher Begg (1986) lists a number of correspondences between Josh 7:1-8:29 and Deut 1:19-3:11. Both open with the sending of spies and their subsequent reports, continue with an attack that leads to disaster, and conclude with a lament before Yahweh. Furthermore, the two texts interpret the events in the same way: the people's disobedience provokes Yahweh to anger so that he is no longer with them. Each case results in a confession of sin and the elimination of the offenders, which makes possible a new attack, initiated by a word from Yahweh, leading to victory.

I refer the reader to Begg's article for a summary of correspondences with Deut 9:7-10:11.

25. While not explicitly stated, selection is made presumably by the casting of lots, thus rendering a sardonic prolepsis to the allotment of territories later in the book.

26. In a deft display of textual prestidigitation, Soggin (1972) removes 8:30-35 from its context and places it after Josh 24:1-27! See also Mayes (1983:51-57).

27. Butler (1983) details correspondences in Deuteronomy.

28. The MT reads "man of Israel." The phrase should probably be regarded as a collective term designating the leaders of Israel, the military, or even the entire congregation. For a discussion of this issue, see Grintz (1966:119) and Butler (1983:101).

29. The language of obeisance, as well as other elements of the episode, indicates a vassal treaty. See the historical studies of Fensham (1964:96-100) and Grintz (1966:113-126).

30. Other readers have been skeptical about the ease with which the Gibeonites pull off their ruse. See Jacob Liver (1963:227), who is not convinced of deception here. Liver, however, attributes the ambivalence to the reworking of an original source that related a peaceful treaty with Gibeon.

31. The situation represents the Wilderness motif turned "upside down" (Butler 1983:104).

32. See Grintz (1966:120-124). Michael Fishbane (1985:207) points out the humor involved in Canaanites using biblical law so as to circumvent it, and the irony in Joshua's decision to apply to the Gibeonites the consequences of the law they themselves have cited.

33. The Gibeonites' defense paraphrases the Deuteronomic credo (Butler 1983:104).

34. For a more detailed study of the correspondences between Deuteronomy 29 and Joshua 9, see Kearney (1973:1-8).

NOTES TO CHAPTER 5:
INTEGRITY AND FRAGMENTATION

1. Thompson (1981) analyzes in detail the passage's mythic dimensions.

2. Polzin (1980:92) notes: "Because the world of ritual can be so clearly demarcated as to its beginning and its end, the liturgical narrative is especially appropriate as an important framing device of the Book of Joshua."

3. Historical critics see the incoherence as evidence of an amalgamation of various recensions or versions of the crossing. For a discussion of textual incongruities, see Soggin (1972:50-67) and Butler (1983:41-51).

4. The MT displays an intriguing alternative (ketibh) at this point, reading 'ad-'avarnu. This indicates a first person plural suffix ("until we crossed over"), which brings the reader directly into the action of the episode but also increases the ambiguity; the reader crosses the Jordan with Israel but maintains a Transjordanian perspective!

5. The radical disjunction between Joshua 12 and 13 has been explained in various ways. Mayes (1983:47-48), for example, believes vss. 1b-6 are intrusive and, noting the conditional tone of the passage, attributes them to a later deuteronomistic editor whose concern was to stress Israel's obedience to the law. Butler (1983:146-47) sees two separate collections of material; the first half of the book is built on oral tradition, while the second half displays evidence of literary activity. Kaufmann (1953) argues that Joshua 1-12 merely relates the

effective breaking of Canaanite resistance, allowing Israel to take the rest of the land in gradual fashion.

6. Yahweh's declaration in 13:1 marks the first time since the initial exhortation in 1:11 that there has been any mention of possession of the land.

7. The land as an organizing principle has been elaborated from the standpoint of myth study by Thompson (1981: 343-58) and through the use of structuralist analysis by Jobling (1986:89-134).

8. See Butler (1983:170).

9. For a discussion of the fragmentary nature of the boundaries of the northern tribes, see Soggin (1972:180-82) and Boling (1982: 402-415). An elaboration of the topographical difficulties is offered by Kuschke (1965:102-06).

10. The Joseph tribes speak and are addressed as if they are one person, thus underscoring their correspondence to Caleb. The Josephites use first person singular forms to refer to themselves, while Joshua also refers to them in the singular. The narrator, however, uses the third person plural.

11. I am translating the imperfect verbal form *torish* as an injunctive. Joshua is not merely exhorting. He is reiterating the commandment to dispossess the inhabitants of the land.

12. The narrator explains the situation by noting that Judah took so much territory that the tribe could not settle it all (an intriguing remark in light of Joseph's complaint that its territory is too small).

NOTES TO CHAPTER 6:
ENDINGS AND AMBIGUITY

1. The difficulty in ending the story evidently remained a problem as the book was transmitted and canonized. In the Greek recensions, the opposing plots conclude the book with the report that the Israelites began to worship Astarte and were subsequently delivered into the hands of Eglon, king of Moab; see the discussion in Boling (1982:542-43).

2. In Joshua and Deuteronomy, the verb *nuah* ("rest") signifies the goal of narrative desire (Deut 3:20; 12:10; 25:19; Josh 1:13, 15; 21:44; 23:1). The verb *shaqat* is used synonymously (Josh 11:23; 14:15) to bring a sense of narrative closure.

3. Cf. Butler (1983:245), Weinfeld (1972:332-39), Boling (1982: 509-10).

4. This point is illustrated well by Jobling (1986:102-03). He sees the story of the altar (which he calls Story II) as a redoubling of the

story of the eastern tribe's request to settle in the Transjordan (Story I). The earlier story, initiated in Num 32:1-42 and completed in Josh 22:1-6, tells how the threat posed by the eastern tribes' request for land was resolved by their promise to participate with the other tribes in campaigns in Canaan. Central to both stories is the threat which the Transjordanians represent to Israel's integrity. The connection between the two stories is made by a "very studied reopening" of the first story, so that "a story of a conflict fully and happily resolved becomes a story of a conflict which led to another conflict."

5. The first assembly at Shiloh took place in the presence of the Tent of Meeting, but the Tent of Meeting is not mentioned here. The western tribes do not seem to take the time to consult Yahweh.

6. See Butler (1983:246).

7. Phinehas will also be present when inter-tribal warfare breaks out later (Judg 20:28).

8. For further information on the meaning of this term see Milgrom (1976:236-47).

9. The potential for closure here creates such a powerful effect that many have suggested that the speech formed the conclusion to an earlier edition of the book. See further Mayes (1983:48-51).

10. These "valedictory addresses" have been attributed to the hand of a deuteronomistic editor, who uses them to provide a schematized historical presentation. See Weinfeld (1972:11-14).

11. Cf. Brooks 1984:95-96.

12. See the discussions in Butler (1983:252) and Boling (1982:525). The verb 'br is also used repeatedly to refer to Israel's entry into the land, making its use in this context ironic: Israel crosses (the Jordan) and transgresses.

13. Joshua 24:1-28 has attracted considerable attention, most of which has been interested in what the passage reveals about Israelite worship and the development of Israel's traditions. The bulk of the discussion has been concerned with its composition (Was it incorporated into Joshua as a unit? What relation does it have to Pentateuchal sources?) and its referent (Was there an ancient covenant renewal at Shechem?). For a review of these issues, see Mayes (1983:48-52) and van Seters (1984:141-46).

14. Giblin (1964:51-69) observes a dialogue pattern discernible in verses 14-24, which creates a symmetry through the seven- and twelve-fold repetition of key terms. A seven-fold occurrence of 'amar ("say") corresponds to a another seven-fold repetition of "Joshua" and "people." Both yhwh and 'avad ("serve") are repeated fourteen times, with the seventh and twelfth repetition of each term occurring at

crucial points. Giblin also argues that the "historical prologue" exhibits numerical symmetry as well, although it is less pronounced.

Many have also seen parallels between Joshua 24 and narrative covenant forms common throughout the Near East. Muilenberg (1959:347-65) discerned stylistic features in various biblical passages which pointed to an ancient literary form used by Israel in ceremonies of covenant renewal. Balzer (1971:19-27) and others have noted parallels between the structures of Joshua 24 and ancient Near Eastern treaties. Baltzer compares Joshua 24 with Hittite treaties and finds a number of intriguing similarities in form and content. This view has been challenged by McCarthy (1978), who sees in Joshua 24 evidence of a pre-Deuteronomistic covenant formulary.

15. Perhaps the reader is given a temporal context in 23:1-16 in order to understand Joshua's words as the completion of a particular era. The information that the book's central figure is "old and advanced in days" signifies that the words he gives provide a concluding frame for the era. The geographical context given in 24:1 (Shechem), on the other hand, hints at Israel's beginnings and gives it a certain timeless quality, intimating a significance that transcends the boundaries of the immediate temporal context.

16. The review is selective in narrating those events which can be imputed completely to Yahweh's activity. This may be one reason for the omission of the Sinai event. The covenant at Sinai was an event in which Israel also played an active role. It therefore does not fit within the pattern of the review, which presents Israel's story in terms of Yahweh's activity and Israel's relative passivity.

NOTES TO CHAPTER 7:
CONCLUSION

1. Cf. Exod 13:5; 33:1-3; Deut 8:1; 10:11; 19:8-9.

2. Exod 23:20-30; 33:1-3; Deut 1:30; 7:22-24; 9:1-5; 11:22-25.

3. For a fuller discussion, see Weinfeld (1972:327-28).

4. Exod 20:3; 23:13, 24, 32-33; 34:15-16; Deut 4:23-24; 6:13-15; 7:14; 8:18-19; 11:16, 28; 12:29-31; 13:1ff; 28:14; 29:17, 25-28; 30:17-18; 31:15-18).

BIBLIOGRAPHY

Alt, Albrecht. 1953. "Das System der Stammesgrenzen im Buche Josua." In *Kleine Schriften I*. München: Beck. Pp. 193-202.

Alter, Robert. 1981. *The Art of Biblical Narrative*. New York: Basic Books.

Aristotle. *The Poetics*. In *Criticism: The Major Statements*, Charles Kaplan, ed. 1986. New York: St. Martins.

Auld, A. Graeme. 1980. *Joshua, Moses and the Land: Tetrateuch-Pentateuch-Hexateuch in a Generation since 1938*. Edinburgh: Clark.

Baltzer, Klaus. 1971. *The Covenant Formulary*. David E. Green, trans. Philadelphia: Fortress.

Bar-Efrat, Shimon. 1989. *Narrative Art in the Bible*. Bible and Literature 17. D. Shefer-Vanson, trans. Sheffield: Almond.

Barth, Christoph. 1971. "Die Antwort Israels." In *Probleme biblischer Theologie*, H. W. Wolff, ed. München: Kaiser.

Begg, Christopher T. 1986. "The Function of Josh. 7:1-8:29 in the Deuteronomistic History." *Biblica* 67:320-34.

Berlin, Adele. 1983. *Poetics and Interpretation of Biblical Narrative*. Bible and Literature 9. Sheffield: Almond.

Bird, Phyllis. 1989. "The Harlot as Heroine: Narrative Art and Social Presupposition in Three Old Testament Texts." *Semeia* 46:119-140.

Boling, Robert G. 1982. *Joshua*. Anchor Bible. New York: Doubleday.

Brams, Steven J. 1980. *Biblical Games: A Strategic Analysis of Stories in the Old Testament*. Cambridge, Mass.: M.I.T.

Brooks, Peter. 1984. *Reading for the Plot*. New York: Random House.

—— 1987. "The Idea of a Psychoanalytic Literary Criticism." In *Discourse in Psychoanalysis and Literature*, S. Rimmon-Kenan, ed. London: Methuen.

Brueggemann, Walter. 1968. "The Kerygma of the Deuteronomistic Historian." *Interpretation* 22:387-402.

—— 1977. *The Land*. Overtures to Biblical Theology 1. Philadelphia: Fortress.

Butler, Trent C. 1983. *Joshua*. Word Biblical Commentary. Waco, Texas: Word Books.

Campbell, K.M. 1972. "Rahab's Covenant." *Vetus Testamentum* 22:243-44.

Chatman, Seymour. 1978. *Story and Discourse*. Ithaca: Cornell Univ.

Childs, Brevard S. 1979. *Introduction to the Old Testament as Scripture*. Philadelphia: Fortress.

Clark, Warren M. 1964. "The Origin and Development of the Land Promise Theme in the Old Testament." Unpub. Ph.D. diss., Yale Univ.

Clines, David J.A. 1978. *The Theme of the Pentateuch*. JSOT Supplement 10. Sheffield: JSOT.

Coats, George W. 1985. "An Exposition for the Conquest Theme?" *Catholic Biblical Quarterly* 47:47-54.

—— 1987. "The Book of Joshua: Heroic Saga or Conquest Theme?" *Journal for the Study of the Old Testament* 38:15-32.

Cross, Frank Moore. 1956. "The Boundary and Province Lists of the Kingdom of Judah." *Journal of Biblical Literature* 75:202-26.

Culley, Robert C. 1984. "Stories of Conquest: Joshua 2, 6, 7 and 8." *Hebrew Annual Review* 8:25-44.

Diepold, Peter. 1972. *Israels Land*. Beiträge zur Wissenschaft vom Alten und Neuen Testament 15. Stuttgart: Kohlhammer.

Dipple, Elizabeth. 1970. *Plot*. The Critical Idiom 12. London: Methuen.

Eagleton, Terry. 1983. *Literary Theory: An Introduction*. Minneapolis: Univ. of Minnesota.

Egan, Kieran. 1978. "What Is a Plot?" *New Literary History* 9:455-73.

Elliger, K. "Tribes, Territories Of." *The Interpreter's Dictionary of the Bible*. Nashville: Abingdon. 4:701-10.

Eslinger, Lyle. 1989. *Into the Hands of the Living God*. Bible and Literature 24. Sheffield: Almond.

Fensham, Charles. 1964. "The Treaty between Israel and the Gibeonites. *Biblical Archaeologist* 27:96-100.

Fishbane, Michael. 1985. *Biblical Interpretation in Ancient Israel*. Oxford: Clarendon.

Genette, Girard. 1980. *Narrative Discourse*. Ithaca: Cornell Univ.

Giblin, C. H. 1964. "Structural Patterns in Jos 24, 1-25." *Catholic Biblical Quarterly* 26:50-69.

Ginzberg, Louis. 1909. *The Legends of the Jews*. Vol IV. Philadelphia: Jewish Publication Society of America.

Gray, John. 1967. *Joshua, Judges and Ruth*. New Century Bible. London: Nelson.

Greenberg, Moshe. 1959. "The Biblical Concept of Asylum." *Journal of Biblical Literature* 78:125-32.

Grintz, Jehoshua M. 1966. "The Treaty of Joshua with the Gibeonites." *Journal of the American Oriental Society* 86:113-26.

Gunn, David M. 1987a. "Joshua and Judges." In *The Literary Guide to the Bible*, Robert Alter & Frank Kermode, eds. Cambridge, Mass.: Belknap/Harvard. Pp. 102-121.

—— 1987b. "New Directions in the Study of Hebrew Narrative." *Journal for the Study of the Old Testament* 39:65-74.

Hamlin, John. 1983. *Inheriting the Land*. International Theological

Commentary. Grand Rapids: Eerdmans/Edinburgh: Handsel.

Iser, Wolfgang. 1978. *The Act of Reading*. Baltimore: Johns Hopkins.

Jobling, David. 1986. *The Sense of Biblical Narrative II: Structural Analyses in the Hebrew Bible*. JSOT Supplement 39. Sheffield: JSOT.

Kallai, Zechariah. 1972. "Tribes, Territories Of." *The Interpreter's Dictionary of the Bible. Supplementary Volume*. Nashville: Abingdon. Pp. 920-23.

Kaufmann, Yehezkel. 1953. *The Biblical Account of the Conquest of Palestine*. M. Dagut, trans. Jerusalem: Magnes.

Kearney, Peter J. 1973. "The Role of the Gibeonites in the Deuteronomic History." *Catholic Biblical Quarterly* 35:1-19.

Kermode, Frank. 1966. *The Sense of an Ending: Studies in the Theory of Fiction*. London: Oxford.

——— 1979. *The Genesis of Secrecy: On the Interpretation of Narrative*. Cambridge, Mass.: Harvard Univ.

——— 1983. "Secrets and Narrative Sequence." In *The Art of Telling: Essays on Fiction*. Cambridge, Mass.: Harvard Univ.

Kloppenborg, John S. 1981. "Joshua 22: The Priestly Editing of an Ancient Tradition." *Biblica* 62:347-71.

Kort, Wesley A. 1988. *Story, Text, and Scripture: Literary Interests in Biblical Narrative*. University Park, Pa.: Penn State.

Kuschke, Arnulf. 1965. "Historisch-topographische Beiträge zum Buch Josue." In *Gottes Wort und Gottes Land*, H. Graf Reventlow, ed. Göttingen: Vandenhoeck & Ruprecht.

Langlamet, F. 1971. "Josue, II, et les traditions de l'Hexateuque." *Revue Biblique* 78:5-17, 161-83, 321-54.

Liver, Jacob. 1963. "The Literary History of Joshua IX." *Journal of Semitic Studies* 8:227-43.

Lohfink, Norbert. "hrm." In *Theological Dictionary of the Old Testament*, G. J. Botterweck and H. Ringgren, eds. Grand Rapids: Eerdmans. 4:180-99.

McCarthy, D. J. 1971a. "The Theology of Leadership in Joshua 1-9." *Biblica* 52:165-75.

——— 1971b. "Some Holy War Vocabulary in Joshua 2." *Catholic Biblical Quarterly* 33:228-30.

——— 1978. *Treaty and Covenant*. Analecta Biblica 21A. Rome: Pontifical Biblical Institute.

McKenzie, John J. 1966. *The World of the Judges*. Englewood Cliffs, N.J.: Prentice-Hall.

Magness, J. Lee. 1986. *Sense and Absence: Structure and Suspension in Mark's Gospel*. Atlanta: Scholars.

Martin, W. J. 1968. " 'Dischronologized' Narrative in the Old Testament." *Vetus Testamentum Supplement* 17:179-86.

Mayes, A. D. H. 1983. *The Story of Israel between Settlement and Exile*. London: SCM.

Milgrom, Jacob. 1976. "The Concept of *Ma'al* in the Bible and the Ancient Near East." *Journal of the American Oriental Society* 96:236-47.

Miller, J. Maxwell and Gene M. Tucker. 1974. *The Book of Joshua.* Cambridge Bible Commentary. Cambridge: Cambridge Univ.

Miller, Patrick D. 1969. "The Gift of God: The Deuteronomic Theology of the Land." *Interpretation* 23:451-65.

Muilenberg, James. 1959. "The Form and Structure of the Covenantal Formulations." *Vetus Testamentum* 9:347-65.

Noth, Martin. 1967. *Überlieferungsgeschichtliche Studien.* 3rd ed. Tübingen: Niemeyer. [1981. *The Deuteronomistic History.* JSOT Supplement 15, J. Doull *et al.*, trans. Sheffield: JSOT.]

Polzin, Robert. 1980. *Moses and the Deuteronomist: A Literary Study of the Deuteronomistic History.* New York: Seabury.

Rad, Gerhard von. 1966. "The Promised Land and Yahweh's Land." In *The Problem of the Hexateuch and Other Essays*, E. W. Trueman Dicken, trans. London: SCM.

Ricoeur, Paul. 1975. "Biblical Hermeneutics." *Semeia* 4:29-148.

―― 1978. "The Narrative Function." *Semeia* 13:177-202.

―― 1980. "Narrative Time." *Critical Inquiry* 7:169-90.

―― 1984. *Time and Narrative. Volume 1.* Kathleen McLaughlin and David Pellauer, trans. Chicago: Univ. of Chicago.

Rimmon-Kenan, Shlomith. 1983. *Narrative Fiction: Contemporary Poetics.* London: Methuen.

Saydon, Paul. 1950. "The Crossing of the Jordan." *Catholic Biblical Quarterly* 12:194-207.

Schafer, Roy. 1980. "Narrative in Psychoanalytic Dialogue." *Critical Inquiry* 7:29-53.

Scholes, Robert and Robert Kellogg. 1966. *The Nature of Narrative.* New York: Oxford.

Smend, Rudolph. 1971. "Das Gesetz und die Völker: ein Beitrag zur deuteronomistischen Redaktionsgeschichte." In *Probleme biblischer Theologie*, H. W. Wolff, ed. München: Kaiser.

Soggin, J. Alberto. 1972. *Joshua.* Old Testament Library. R. A. Wilson, trans. Philadelphia: Westminster.

Spence, Donald. 1982. *Narrative Truth and Historical Truth: Meaning and Interpretation in Psychanalysis.* New York: Norton.

Sternberg, Meir. 1985. *The Poetics of Biblical Narrative: Ideological Literature and the Drama of Reading.* Indiana Literary Biblical Series. Bloomington: Indiana Univ.

Thompson, Leonard L. 1981. "The Jordan Crossing: *Sidqot* Yahweh and World Building." *Journal of Biblical Literature* 100:343-58.

Tucker, Gene. 1972. "The Rahab Saga (Joshua 2): Some Form Critical and Traditio-Critical Observations." In *The Use of the Old Testament in the New and Other Essays*, J. M. Efird, ed. Durham, N.C.: Duke Univ.

Van Seters, John. 1984. "Joshua 24 and the Problem of Tradition in the Old Testament." In *In the Shelter of Elyon*, W. B. Barrick and J. Spencer, eds. JSOT Supplement 31. Sheffield: JSOT. Pp. 139-158.

Wagner, Siefried. 1964. "Die Kundschaftergeschichten im Alten Testament." *Zeitschrift für die altestamentliche Wissenschaft* 76: 255-69.

Waldo, Hans Eberhard von. 1974. "Israel and Her Land: Some Theological Considerations." In *A Lamp Unto My Path: Old Testament Studies in Honor of Jacob M. Meyers*. Philadelphia: Temple Univ.

Weinfeld, Moshe. 1967. "The Period of the Conquest and the Judges as Seen in the Earlier and the Later Sources." *Vetus Testamentum* 17:97-113.

—— 1972. *Deuteronomy and the Deuteronomic School*. Oxford: Clarendon.

Wenham, Gordon J. 1971. "The Deuteronomic Theology of the Book of Joshua." *Journal of Biblical Literature* 90:40-48.

Westermann, Claus. 1984. *Genesis 1-11*. J. J. Scullion, trans. Minneapolis: Augsburg.

White, Haydon. 1980. "The Value of Narrativity in the Representation of Reality." *Critical Inquiry* 7:5-27.

Wilcoxen, J. A. 1968. "Narrative Structure and Cult Legend: A Study of Joshua 1-6." In *Transitions in Biblical Scholarship*, J. C. Rylaarsdam, ed. Chicago: Univ. of Chicago.

Wolff, Hans Walter. "Das Kerygma des deuteronomistischen Geschichtswerk." *Zeitschrift für die altestamentliche Wissenschaft* 73:171-86. ["The Kerygma of the Deuteronomic Historical Work." Frederick C. Prussner, trans. In *The Vitality of Old Testament Traditions*, W. Brueggemann and H. W. Wolff, eds. Atlanta: John Knox.]

Woudstra, Martin H. 1980. *The Book of Joshua*. New International Commentary on the Old Testament. Grand Rapids: Eerdmans.

Wright, Elizabeth. 1987. "Transmission in Psychoanalysis and Literature: Whose Text Is It Anyway?" In *Discourse in Psychoanalysis and Literature*, S. Rimmon-Kenan, ed. London: Methuen.

Wright, G. Ernest. 1982. "Introduction." In *Joshua*. Anchor Bible. New York: Doubleday.

Zimmerli, Walther. 1960. "Promise and Fulfillment." In *Essays on Old Testament Hermeneutics*. C. Westermann, ed. J. L. Mays, trans. Richmond: John Knox.

INDEXES

AUTHORS

SUBJECTS

BIBLICAL REFERENCES